Church on the Edge of Somewhere

Church on the Edge of Somewhere

Ministry, Marginality, and the Future

George B. Thompson, Jr.

Foreword by Lovett H. Weems, Jr.

THE
ALBAN
INSTITUTE

Herndon, Virginia
www.alban.org

The Alban Institute
2121 Cooperative Way, Suite 100
Herndon, VA 20171

Scripture quotations, unless otherwise noted, are from the New Revised Standard Version of the Bible, © 1989, Division of Christian Education of the National Council of Churches of Christ in the United States of America, and are used by permission.

Cover design by Spark Design, LLC.

Library of Congress Cataloging-in-Publication Data

Thompson, George B. (George Button), 1951-
  Church on the edge of somewhere : ministry, marginality, and the
      future / George B. Thompson, Jr.
    p. cm.
  Includes bibliographical references.
  ISBN-13: 978-1-56699-348-7
  1. Church. I. Title.
  BV600.3.T455 2007
  250--dc22
                            2007035171

11   10   09   08   07   VG   1   2   3   4   5

In grateful memory of Ginger Rogers Kaney (1948-2006),
Decatur, Georgia,
Who followed her vocation among and for
"the least of these,"
Who taught by quiet yet clear example,
Who loved across many lines,
And whose funeral celebrated a rich life,
a deep faith, and gospel witness
of enduring inspiration.

And with inexpressible thanks to Beverly,
A true partner in all the ventures of life.

Contents

Foreword

One of the revitalizing aspects of theological education today is the keen attention given to context. Students are given significant resources to help them observe and understand the cultural context in which they are serving in ministry. They develop a genuine sensitivity to the ways in which a host of contextual factors will shape what faithful and fruitful ministry will look like in those settings. George Thompson, a wise and incisive observer of church life and pastoral leadership, has provided us with another valuable tool for such analysis.

Drawing from his fine scholarship and his lifetime of church experience, Thompson has the ability to translate theoretical concepts into the practical realities of congregational life. Just as important is his desire, even passion, to illustrate what multiple disciplines have to offer to the church's witness and also to show how the church's beliefs and values shape the ways these disciplines are employed within the church.

Churches always stand in relationship with their identity and with their environment. Those churches that thrive take both very seriously. They know who they are and what they believe, and they also are in a vibrant, interactive relationship with their surrounding community. All churches stand in these relationships, but few are deliberate in deciding how they will relate to identity and to environment.

Thompson develops his Contextual Posture Grid around the internal (identity) and external (environment) postures of congregations. Does a congregation focus primarily on those inside the church, or does it focus on those beyond the congregation? And does the congregation view itself "at home" with its surrounding environment or does it see itself as different from the dominant external context? Where churches stand in relationship to their identity and environment places them in various quadrants of Thompson's grid, with corresponding implications for the shape of their ministry and their leadership opportunities and constraints.

While no one approach is right for all churches at all times, some make vital ministry more likely. Thompson makes much of the marginal stance of many churches and sees more promise for vital ministry in marginality than is conventionally imagined. More and more churches today find themselves on the margins. Not only is life on the edge closer to the reality of the New Testament church; we know that marginality has often been associated with creativity and leadership. Both the center and the edge offer opportunities to serve God so long as one never forgets the limitations and temptations of each.

Lovett H. Weems Jr., Director of the Lewis Center for
Church Leadership, Wesley Theological Seminary

CHAPTER 1

Ostriches or Lemonade Stands?

Churches Face a Twenty-First-Century World

Dreaming of the Past

When my daughter was very young, I remember reading a book to her entitled *The Little House*.[1] This charming book tells the story of a house that is built beside a gurgling brook, surrounded by the singing birds in spring and the smells of cider in the fall. As the years go by and more houses are built around it, the little house gradually loses its bucolic setting. The houses become a town, with many streets, shops, and people. The town grows and grows. Before long, rail lines and smokestacks and streetcars appear all around the little house. With skyscrapers towering over it, the house loses almost all of its sunlight. Now the house is empty; its shutters hang crooked, and the paint has peeled off almost completely. Yet no one seems to notice as they drive and walk briskly past the useless little house on their way to work or the shops.

As in many children's books, the story of the little house has something of a fairy tale ending. One day, just as it looks as though the little house might be torn down, a large truck drives up and men surround the house. They dig around its walls and small foundation and bring a large machine close to the little house. The machine lifts the house onto the truck, which then drives the house out of the city for miles and miles until it stops by a quiet hill next to a field and gurgling brook. There, the men from the truck dig a cellar for the little house. Then they place it in its new location. Here once again the birds sing outside of its windows, and a brook gurgles alongside. It is a happy little house once more.

I enjoyed reading this book to my daughter years ago when she was little. Its story begins and ends with a scene that carries tremendous idyllic appeal—of returning to the comfortable and simple roots of a good life, sheltered from the neglect and sometimes threats of a fast-paced world. No wonder that this book, *The Little House*, is still read to children today, more than six decades after its publication. None of us can survive without some hope that, no matter what happens, in the end we will be rescued, we will be safe, we can return to the trouble-free joys of our earliest memories.

Metaphors of Response

Yes, I believe that reading books like *The Little House* to young children is a positive way to nurture them as they are growing up. I wonder, however, whether stories like this one are helpful in the same way once we have become adults. Children's books can be both true and simple—which means that they don't necessarily tell the whole story. Adults know that life is more complex than hoping for every crisis to be solved passively by a rescue. The apostle Paul makes the point, I believe, in his reference to "putting an end to childish ways" in the famous love chapter (1 Corinthians 13:11). Yes, as Paul says, "Love never ends" (1 Corinthians 13:8a), but at the same time, acting like a child can be dangerous for adults. It could lead us into "the ostrich syndrome" of responding to life's challenges by simply sticking our heads in the sand and hoping that it all will go away.

Communities of faith become tempted to act like ostriches, too. What does your congregation do when it perceives a threat? Does it try to pretend that if it can just ignore what is "out there," everything will be fine? Or has it learned how to lean into those moments and situations that confront life in the twenty-first century? It seems more realistic, and even safer, to live by the conviction that the world indeed will change around us and we need to learn to respond. An ostrich with its head in the sand is hardly well prepared to encounter . . . anything! Yet this is the posture that many of our churches assume. They feel like the Little House—surrounded by a world that has grown up around it, and from which it feels the need to be rescued.

When I was in college, I remember seeing a poster in a friend's dormitory room. Its yellow, cartoon-like drawing was intertwined with the words, "When life gives you lemons, make lemonade." For grownups and their churches, this citric metaphor seems more realistic—and useful—than that of the well-intentioned but naïve ostrich. This lemony saying encourages us to look at sour situations in creative ways. Rather than complaining that we don't like the taste in the cup, we instead can make something appealing out of it.

Aims of This Book

It is to the tasks of creative, faithful, and effective congregational ministry that this book turns. You will learn the differences between congregations that act like the little house, those that are like ostriches, and those that see opportunities to run lemonade stands. Here, I introduce you to a language of conversation for making sense out of the increasingly complex worlds in which our churches find themselves. This language helps us as churches to think soberly, yet hopefully, about our calling as God's people, in light of the many lemons of opportunity that appear on today's landscape. Being both sober yet hopeful, the ministry framework I propose in this book finds a fitting place for the Little House scenario while also continuing to encourage churches to build lemonade stands. In other words, there is no one right way to be the church of the future; that approach would be too simplistic. The model of church analysis here frames possibilities in terms that do not polarize options or pit one church or church "posture" against another. At the same time, it will be clear by the end of the book that the demands of the gospel are calling many of today's churches to build new lemonade stands.

Models are tools: they help the user understand something in a new way and they suggest how the new understanding points to fresh possibilities. Before beginning to learn the model itself, however, it will be helpful first to be more specific about why new tools like this one are necessary. We have intimated already that our new century is different than the one we just left. Yet in our churches we often don't see these differences as lemons of opportunity.

Life Gives Your Church Lemons

Life's lemons today show up as we begin to lean into the ambiguities of a future that is less and less conventional. Such ambiguities are easily observable as the American population *becomes more diverse* in all kinds of ways. Perhaps the most obvious evidence of this diversity is in racial and ethnic presence. Visit a local shopping mall and you are likely to see persons from a number of racial and ethnic heritages—black (which could be African, African American, Caribbean, or others), Hispanic (which could be Mexican, Cuban, Central American, South American, or others), Asian (which could be Korean, Filipino, Taiwanese, Thai, or others), Indian (both from the subcontinent and from native American tribes), South Pacific, and others, besides the majority white ethnics of virtually all the European nationalities. These days, this degree of diversity is just as likely in Minneapolis as it is in New York or Los Angeles. Such trends suggest that by the middle of our present century European Americans will lose their majority status, becoming the largest of a number of ethnic categories in a "salad bowl" society.

An ostrich response to increasing diversity would be to ignore new groups that are different from what your congregation already is. So ask yourself: how willing or prepared is your congregation to welcome people from a different racial or ethnic background? For what kind of changes in your church would authentic hospitality call?

A second lemon to a struggling, older congregation might be that this growing, diversifying population is *increasingly concentrated in metropolitan areas.* A century ago, the vast majority of those living in the United States resided in small towns; today, most people live in or near a big city. More precisely, clusters of municipalities, usually surrounding a larger, older city, are increasing in number and in size. The America that in 1900 was still a rural nation is now dominated by cities.[2] The implications of this trend are many. For one thing, it means that people live closer together; the population density is increasing. Physical isolation from others is less likely than it used to be. For another thing, it suggests that even at a superficial level our exposure to people who are ethnically, economically, socially, and culturally different from us occurs more often.

An ostrich response to metropolitan concentration would be to complain about population growth, new subdivisions, crowding, and shopping centers without a serious conversation to understand them. So ask yourself: how has the town or region where your congregation's facilities are located changed since it was founded? To what extent are those changes a part of an ongoing conversation that guides your church's life and witness?

Third, *a "shrinking" effect* across the Earth is being created that involves these other two human trends. Technologies of travel and communication continue to bring people into closer, more frequent, and interactive contact. When I was a child, a medical missionary and his wife visited our church. They had spent years living in Cameroon, West Africa. At my tender age, I could not imagine the time and distance involved in their travels between the two continents. With jet flights now so common, today it is difficult to ignore how practically interconnected the human family has become.

An ostrich response to a shrinking world would be to ignore new technology, either as a tool or as an influence on the daily world which the congregation engages. So ask yourself: to what parts of the United States and the Earth have your church members traveled or lived? What did they do there? How is your congregation influenced by these travels?

A fourth lemon, especially in denominations with European roots, will be the formal governing structures of the United States, which functions as a *representative democracy with no state religion*. The significance of this reality can be appreciated only in the context of history. European nations whose American immigrants gave major shape to the emergence of the fledgling union at the end of the eighteenth century were accustomed to one particular Christian denomination or another as the state church. Anglican/Episcopalian, Lutheran, Presbyterian/Reformed, and Roman Catholic traditions had dominated Europe. Even though certain North American colonies privileged certain denominations, the new United States of America did not allow any religious institution to become an official state religion. Thus, although religious institutions and values always have influenced life, government, and politics in America, they have not enjoyed the same kind of formal privilege historically bestowed upon, say, the Church of England.

An ostrich response to freedom of religion could be maintenance of traditions of privilege, even as your church's members live in a democratic society. So ask yourself: what is your church's historical tradition? Was it a "state church" at one time? How does the American political system influence the way that your church operates? What happens, for instance, if church members who are accustomed to making decisions in their jobs are limited in participation at church by its form of government?

Our fifth and final lemon of opportunity and reality for the twenty-first–century world is the *increasing sense of American insecurity* in the wake of the terrorist attacks on September 11, 2001. Though it has abated somewhat since 2001, this sense of insecurity would likely skyrocket if there were another such attack. Being "American" does not feel as protected as it once did—say, in the wake of the Allied victories of World War II. Americans are not accustomed to viewing themselves as being susceptible to external military threat. The recent history of international terrorist activity now has reached North America, and we as a people are somewhat uneasy.

A church's ostrich response to terrorist insecurity might be to allow our fear and anger to fester quietly, with no biblical and theological reflection, until it explodes irrationally at some other issue. So ask yourself: what public discourse has taken place since September 11, 2001, in your church about terrorism? Of what are your church members afraid? How does their understanding of the Gospel help them deal with these fears?

Location, Location, Location

With life in the twenty-first century handing out these kinds of lemons, what tools will help churches to build lemonade stands for their future? I agree with those who argue that the world which we now inhabit is different enough from the post-World War II era that we have to shift to new paradigms to function in it effectively.[3] In this book, I introduce a model that I call the "contextual posture grid." This four-part grid functions as a tool both for discovery and action. Each one of the four locations on the grid is described in some combination of the terms "middle," "edge," "nowhere," "anywhere," or "somewhere." I dismiss none of the locations, or "postures," out of hand; each one I characterize in such a way that the reasons for a church inhabiting one posture or another make sense. At the same time, the context for this discussion compels us to imagine how churches will respond more fully to the gospel call out of one location in particular. Of the four, it is the one that exhibits an imaginative capacity for dealing with marginality.

Throughout our lives, most of us have encountered—or at least become aware of—persons or communities that were situated outside of whatever informal standard for "fitting in" applied. They might have been the wrong color, or denomination, or nationality, or religion, or education, or income level for your community to fully approve of them as they were. As adults, we tend to accept such standards as they are, for the social factors in which we live operate to shape us in this way. Think about a time when you became especially aware of those who live on the edge of such a standard. How did you perceive them, think about them, treat them? Typically, we are uncomfortable if "they" have crossed over the edge, beyond the line that the "standard" sets.

Typically, we will respond to the existence of edges the same way that an ostrich does when it senses danger.

Connecting with Edges: A Personal Account

I believe that all of us can discover something in our own lives that can give us a feel for what it is like to be left out. In the last two chapters, we will see how learning to get in touch with our own communal edges is a spiritual exercise in church renewal. Allow me to demonstrate this point with myself. As I look back over the years, I realize that I have lived in and with a number of points of marginality. Some of them came and went, some of them remain, and others have appeared more recently.

The Matter at Hand

For instance, I am left-handed. I was born that way, as all true "lefties" are. We constitute only ten percent of the population, which makes us a small minority. We have had to learn to adapt to a world that is run by right-handed people, whose practices and devices almost always leave us out. When I was in third grade, my elderly teacher told us how her son had been forced at school to learn how to write with his right hand. He was naturally left-handed, but the longstanding educational practice was to use physical measures, if necessary, to ensure that lefties became righties. Her son's teacher would strike his left hand with a wooden ruler if he did not pick up a pencil with his right hand. Finally, she tied his left wrist against his belly with a belt.

Fortunately for me and my third-grade teacher's grandson (who was two years younger than me), educational practice concerning "handed-ness" has changed. Ironically, however, I was not given specific instruction on how to write. All the green cards with line drawings above the chalkboard showed a right hand holding and using the pencil. Our teacher gave none of us lefties in the class any instruction. So I looked carefully at the drawing and reversed it in my mind, mentally seeing the left hand holding the pencil. Then I used this image to practice the correct hand posture as I followed the arrows showing how to form each letter. Most lefties whom I have met over the years hold a pen or pencil as though it were in a claw, bending their wrists to a 45-degree angle as they push the pencil across the paper—sometimes even toward themselves, rather than parallel to the body. Yet, even with tolerance among today's schools, left-handed persons still find it inconvenient, annoying, and sometimes downright exasperating to live in a world that is set up for right-handers. As a child, I tried to make lemonade out of the situation.

The Two of Us
My left-handedness, however, was not the first marginal feature about me that people noticed. I am also a twin, an identical twin at that. My brother and I looked almost exactly alike as babies and children; people still mistake us for each other today. Yes, we are both left-handed! Twins occur in only about one of 88 births, and identical twins are even less common. Being a twin was probably my first label of identity, one given to me by the nature of my birth. Robert and I grew up drawing attention in public, being fawned over by elderly relatives, being constantly compared to each other. In older grades, we quietly competed with each other and gave up the pranks (our friends could tell us apart, so we could not foil the other one's social pursuits!). After a while, the attention did not feel that positive. We were left-handed twins, but we both got to the point of just wanting to fit in. Privately, I liked both of my unusual features, but eventually I had to ignore them to pursue my goals. The ostrich won that round.

Journeys Off the Path
Besides being born a left-handed twin, I have had a number of life experiences with being on edges. Some of them were as a result of my choices, but others cannot be viewed that way so easily. The state in which I grew up, Oregon, is in the geographically remote northwest corner of the United States. In terms of news that would draw national attention, Oregon was off the radar. Nelson Rockefeller visited my home town briefly when he was running for president in 1964 (my parents did not let me leave school to see him), and the popular 1950s singer Johnnie Ray grew up there. Neither of these claims gave my hometown

or my state any fame as a desirable place to live. It certainly was not anyone's New York, Chicago, or California.

Like many towns in Oregon, mine survived on an economy driven by farming and logging. I was the studious type, though, and even though I got pretty good in summer baseball and played basketball at school, I felt out of place most of the time. My activities in student government seemed only to distance me further from my classmates. Then I chose to attend college near Seattle, but during those years I ended up going into the city only a handful of times. Virtually all of my time and energy outside of class were channeled into a loosely affiliated group of religious students who viewed ourselves as the true believers. We just knew that we were "real Christians," and we were skeptical of other students who went to church without the passion and perspectives that we promoted. The college was small enough for me to have become involved in a number of activities, but I was too busy being a real Christian to involve myself with "worldly" matters. After I graduated from college, I became a little more active at seminary, but I chose to attend one that was not sponsored by my denomination. Years later, I began to realize that I had very few ongoing relationships with other pastors in my denomination because I had had almost no connections with them while at seminary.

When I was ordained and began to serve congregations, any friendships and collegial relationships were difficult to establish and maintain. Much of the reason was my mobility. First, I moved 1,200 miles from the seminary to serve a church in a farm town on the plains of Colorado, which had a large Hispanic population that no one at church ever discussed. Next, I moved a thousand miles in another direction, to serve a smaller church in an even smaller town in the southern part of my home state. My third pastoral move was 2,500 miles long, in yet another direction. Living near Chicago was both stimulating and disorienting. There were many aspects of Midwestern life that were new and puzzling to me. During these pastoral years, I also discovered that my passion for Christian education was very low on the priority list of most clergy whom I met, no matter where I lived. Two of my pastoral experiences were with congregations outside of my denomination. My earliest teaching experiences in higher education were in Catholic colleges or with a student body that was heavily Catholic. My first full-time labor in theological education was with a seminary not of my denomination. During those years, I lived in the city of Chicago—a long journey for someone who grew up in a farm-and-mill town 50 miles from the Pacific Ocean, where the coastal temperatures rarely moved above 72 degrees.

Reflections from Edges

More than once during those years, these experiences with many kinds of marginality left me feeling in the middle of nowhere. Even though I was trying to follow God's calling on my life, it was difficult in many of these situations to believe that I was accomplishing anything that had to do with my call. If you'd asked me then, I wouldn't have been convinced that I was able to make lemonade. My sense of where "somewhere" was—that is, the world's opinion of a desired place and its accompanying activities—seemed most of the time to me to be quite distant from where I was or what I was able to do.

It took a number of years for me to realize that I have lived with and around many different kinds of edges. One could argue that the decisions to make the geographical moves were fully mine, and to a large extent, this is true. Yet I rarely was able to anticipate the challenges that the new locations presented. The geographical change, then, only symbolized the edginess of the new opportunity. It is usually no fun to feel in the middle of nowhere.

Yet now, at this point in my life, edges and nowheres have taken on a biblical and theological meaning that was difficult to appropriate in those earlier years. I have come to realize that our biblical ancestors—including Jesus, no less—were very familiar with the realities to which these metaphors of location allude. Indeed, I even preached a sermon early in my first days living near Chicago about Abraham as my spiritual guide. What I could not understand then was that these many journeys among seeming nowheres have developed in me a sensitivity that I never would have acquired otherwise. It is an awareness of marginality—of edges—that the world around us defines on its own terms and of the people who inhabit them.

The twenty-first century will continue to create many edges in many ways. To most people who read this book, edges appear as a change or threat of change, sour and unappealing to the palate. Our churches are no less susceptible to feeling repelled by edges than a large business in an economy where the rules have changed or a city with a growing population of "foreigners." Yet as the dormitory room poster read, "When life gives you lemons, make lemonade." I believe that one way to pose the primary challenge to churches today is with this simple-sounding adage. Surely God's people, with its biblical heritage of calling, wandering, wondering, rescue, threat, conquest, settlement, stagnation, and so on, can discover faithful ways to build lemonade stands at the edges of their changing worlds.

What to Expect

In the pages and chapters that follow, you will learn a theory of congregational life that will be new to you.[4] I outline it in chapter 2. You will see each part of the model elaborated and illustrated by reference to stories from congregations in chapters 3, 4, 5, and 6. Figures and diagrams in each chapter will help you visualize each posture and their relationships to each other. Along the way, we will use insights from the Bible, sociology, and cultural anthropology to reflect on the model's main concepts (especially "edge," "marginality," and "empathy"). Toward the end of the book, we will consider two particular congregations whose stories and ministries underscore our primary emphasis. Not least, we will reflect on these various congregational postures in terms of leadership. Chapter 7 considers how congregations can and do move from one location to another, and what it looks like to lead such moves. By the end of the book, I hope that you will not only have learned a new tool, but that you also are inspired to help any ostriches in your church learn how to build lemonade stands wherever they find themselves.

Hearing Old Voices Again

As theories go, this contextual posture grid is new, even though the conditions and dynamics that it seeks to explain are not. When I lived in Chicago, I became interested in the legacy of Jane Addams, whose work as a social reformer and international peace advocate is still highly regarded. In 1913, at a time when Addams' reputation had grown significantly, the settlement house pioneer wrote an introduction to a book that today is obscure. *Religion in Social Action* was written by a Rev. Graham Taylor, a diligent pastor who spent much of his life as a ground-breaking seminary professor. One thing that distinguished Taylor's work was his decision early in his teaching career at The Chicago Theological Seminary to purchase a house not far from campus and turn it into a settlement house, much like Jane Addams' Hull House. Not only this, Taylor's own seminary students lived in this house as well. While studying the Bible, theology, ethics, and church history, these students were among the first ever to learn what was called "Christian sociology." The living laboratory of "Chicago Commons," located "in one of those shifting city districts to which people of a score of nationalities are drawn from all parts of the world,"[5] taught the students more than mere social theories.

Addams was impressed with Professor Taylor's "unfaltering courage"[6] in his "attempt to connect religious enthusiasm with civic and economic needs."[7] For more than two decades, Taylor's students were challenged to prepare themselves to help their future congregations make this same connection. In so doing, they would be inviting those churches to live on some kind of an edge, resourcefully and creatively. This was not an easy posture to promote or maintain, yet its links to the Gospel are undeniable.

Now, a century later, the future of many of our own congregations is uncertain. Perhaps we have forgotten what Jane Addams and Graham Taylor tried to show the churches of their day. Perhaps the time has come to listen to them afresh. This book is one effort to help Christians and their congregations

hear the ancient call to faith and witness in a new way, for a
new time.

Notes

1. Virginia Lee Burton, story and pictures, *The Little House* (Boston:
   Houghton Mifflin, 1942), which won the coveted Caldecott Medal
   in 1943 for artwork in a children's book.
2. For a quick look at information on U.S. cities, see "Demographics of the United States" on the Wikipedia Web site, http://
   en.wikipedia.org/wiki/Demographics_of_the_United_States (accessed 28 December 2006). This site notes the ten largest U.S. cities, their metropolitan populations and rank, population densities
   for a number of U.S. cities (Manhattan has over 66,000 residents
   per square mile!), race, religious affiliation, income and so on.
3. Joel Barker's Web site, www.joelbarker.com (accessed 27 December 2006), outlines his ground-breaking contribution to the discussion of paradigm shifts.
4. Models of church are not new. Several books have offered either
   normative or descriptive models of congregational style, while
   secular authors have developed organizational models with use-
   fulness for churches. Avery Dulles's *Models of the Church* (expand-
   ed edition, New York: Image Books/Doubleday, 1987), describes
   five religious models: institution, mystical communion, sacra-
   ment, herald, servant. These models are ecclesiological, present-
   ing theologically based interpretations. Dulles, a Jesuit, also has
   read carefully in both Protestant and social scientific thought, but
   his discussion does not focus on the parish or local church.
   Sociology of religion has produced various ways to frame religious organizations. David A. Roozen, William McKinney, and
   Jackson W. Carroll's volume, *Varieties of Religious Presence: Mission
   in Public Life* (New York: The Pilgrim Press, 1984) acknowledges
   the work of Dulles, as well as major earlier sociological and theological discussions by Weber, Troeltsch and H. Richard Niebuhr,.
   Their model focuses upon mission in particular rather than the
   congregation in general. The four "mission orientations" that they
   designate are *activist*, *civic*, *sanctuary*, and *evangelistic*. The authors
   created these orientations based upon two sets of distinctions that
   emerged from their research. One distinction is between the con-

gregation's interest in the world beyond or the world here—"other-worldly" versus "this-worldly." The other distinction is between the congregation's attitude toward involvement in the wider public arena: is it proactive or resistant? *Varieties* is a well-written, scholarly work.

Four-part models like the one in *Varieties,* that are illustrated by quadrants, appear elsewhere in secular literatures, too. Business management consultants Deal and Kennedy (Terrence E. Deal and Allen A. Kennedy, *Corporate Cultures: The Rites and Rituals of Corporate Life,* Reading: Addison-Wesley, 1982) developed a grid for corporate business cultures that is based upon two factors: degree of *risk* (low vs. high) and speed of *feedback* (slow vs. fast). Deal and Kennedy argue that each one of the quadrants represents a distinctive type of corporate culture. In a similar structural vein, R. Stephen Warner (*New Wine in Old Wineskins: Evangelicals and Liberals in a Small-Town Church,* Berkeley: University of California Press, 1988, ch. 2, esp. 34–36) developed in his sociological study of a Presbyterian church a "cultural map of American Protestantism." One axis of the quadrant measures *form* (nascent vs. institutional); the other axis measures *content* (evangelical vs. liberal). Warner, like others who develop typologies, points out that the distinctions in such quadrants are relative to "internally diverse" dynamics within churches. In other words, the purpose of typologies is not to 'pigeon-hole' organizations but to identify observable trends and characteristics that apply to congregations as a whole.

Dudley and Johnson's five-part typology of American congregations (Carl A. Dudley and Sally A. Johnson, *Energizing the Congregation: Images that Shape Your Church's Ministry,* Louisville: Westminster John Knox Press, 1993) is more like Dulles's ecclesiological framework. Like *Varieties,* the Dudley/Johnson typology is based upon an extensive empirical research project, which emerged out of the Center for Church and Community Ministry. The model itself is described in rather concise terms; much of the book's text is narrative, drawing from case studies of project congregations. This book is written for a lay audience, designed to be used by congregations.

Joseph McCann's *Church and Organization: A Sociological and Theological Enquiry,* Scranton: University of Scranton Press/Associated University Presses, 1993) provides a broad discussion of organizational theory, sociology, and ecclesiology as it offers a cube-shaped (i.e., with eight interrelated categories) model of church. McCann draws heavily from secular theorists in constructing the cube, which he then uses to analyze the Hartford study typology from *Varieties*. For those interested in theory as well as theology, this book is very enlightening. For an audience of practitioners, it would intimidate.

In her recent book, *The Practicing Congregation: Imagining a New Old Church* (Herndon, VA: The Alban Institute, 2004), Diana Butler Bass offers yet another model, as she writes of great potential for church renewal. It is based on a research project of fifty congregations in seven mainline denominations. By learning to redefine themselves imaginatively, mainline congregations, Bass argues, can become "intentional" about their "practices." Such "practicing congregations" thus offer a new paradigm.

As a live alternative for mainline Protestantism, the practicing congregation contributes to an analytical model of churches that Bass calls a "multidimensional grid." This grid is made up of three intersecting continua: between "established" and "conservative" on one; between "liberal" and "conservative" on another; and on a third dimension, the categories of "postliberal" and "postevangelical" both moving toward the "intentional" end. These three interacting categories, Bass posits, will be useful for explaining historical and theological patterns among many American congregations, as well as pointing to positive new trends.

5. Jane Addams, "Introduction," in Graham Taylor, *Religion in Social Action*, (New York: Dodd, Mead & Company, 1913), xxv.

6. Ibid.

7. Ibid., xxxiv.

CHAPTER 2

Finding Your Church on the Map

A View from the Road

Imagine that you are on a long car trip. Some of the time, you are able to drive on freeways, where your view is limited to exit and mileage signs, clusters of gas stations, restaurants and motels, and perhaps farms or an occasional industrial structure. The rest of the time, your destination requires that you take highways right through populated areas, into the middle of towns. These sections of your trip certainly slow you down, but they also provide an opportunity to get a flavor of some of the communities along the way.

Perhaps like me you pay some attention to the churches in these communities. Perhaps, on the outskirts of town, before the city limit sign comes into view, you will see a simple structure with a cross on the roof. It is a plain building, recently constructed, with light blue aluminum siding and a white sign in block black letters written in Spanish. An adjacent open piece of land bears tire marks in the ground. As you drive into town, you might notice a traditional-looking church building a block or two off the highway that will take you eventually through downtown. It is a wooden structure, several decades in age, with signs both of wear and of recent upkeep. Modest houses surround it on all sides, parking is limited, and a playground with climbing toys for preschoolers sits adjacent to the church's back door. This church's sign might include the words "Missionary Baptist" on it.

By the time you have driven into town, there is a good chance that you will have passed one or perhaps two large, stone church buildings—the kind reminiscent of European cathedrals, with huge, thick, double front doors, high and elaborate roof lines, and carefully tended landscaping. Such buildings exude an air of permanence and strength. Their signs are lighted marquees, with the pastor's name listed as "Dr." and a list of weekly activities that could make one's head spin. These days, you might also see another sign somewhere on this impressive church's property. Unlike the marquee, however, this sign is completely indecipherable to most of us who are familiar at best with the alphabets of languages with European origin. You would be on target to assume that here a population of persons with roots far across many oceans is being invited to gather.

What might these brief glimpses at houses of worship on your drive through town suggest about the congregations who inhabit them?

Clues to Cultural Soul

The academic discipline of sociology can help students of religion identify various patterns in the way that human communities organize themselves as religious bodies. Certainly, buildings cannot tell the whole story of the people who assemble there. But real estate and location do provide hints.

We would be making a good guess, for instance, that the Spanish sign in front of the aluminum-sided building on the edge of town represents a Hispanic congregation. This church might not be very old, we surmise, as we recall news articles about the increasing immigration of Latin Americans to the United States. The modesty of the structure itself might represent the overall social and economic position of the church's members, in contrast to other populations in town. This guess on your part would be substantiated in part by the presence of the large stone church. The Spanish-speaking church members probably have lived in this town for less than a generation. They are likely to be employed as day laborers, doing simple, routine jobs for modest wages. Most of the women in this community are busy raising children and caring for homes, most of which are rented. Their children often huddle together on the playground at school and eat in one corner of the cafeteria. The younger ones can speak English without a trace of accent, but the teenagers are more self-conscious of the way that they speak and dress, of their skin color and their parents' occupations.

We can imagine further that this church plays a central role in the lives of its members, serving as a haven, a safe, sacred space away from the daily pressures of work, school, and home-making. In many ways, this church community is a stranger in a strange land, driven by economic necessity, between a world that it knew well to one that is unfamiliar and often not hospitable. Have any of us ever gone through such an experience? We would yearn for signs of home, of something that we treasure, of being accepted on our own terms. The promise of the Gospel comforts us and gives us hope that life will be better because of God.

In this same town are other churches. A little off the beaten path sits the facility of the Baptist congregation. It is located in a part of town that the majority of the residents implicitly understand to be designated to "them." When the congregation was first organized, Jim Crow laws limited the activities of the neighborhood's residents severely. Their skin color was a constant reminder of an economic system built on the backs of their ancestors, of a war that wiped out a generation of men, of substandard school buildings, of signs posted over water fountains and public restrooms. These days, the residents of this neighborhood shop in the same grocery stores and retail shops as everyone else. They can buy new cars at the same auto dealers. The houses along the narrow streets in the neighborhood have a simple yet decided sparkle to them. In recent years, the congregation has grown considerably, in membership, activity, and influence. Its pastor wears a handsome suit most days and no longer works a second job. City Council, law enforcement officers, and other civic officials talk regularly with him about issues affecting the community. Church members are proud of their pastor.

Everyone in town, however, knows that if you want to show that you have "arrived," *the* church to join is the one right downtown. It was the first congregation established there, five years before municipal incorporation. Its history is interlaced closely with the growth of the town that became a small city. More than-half of the town's mayors have held membership at the old stone church and certain civic and cultural events are still held in the church's facilities. When a new social issue emerges in the public arena, this congregation has been the first to respond—with a food bank, clothes closet, day care center, night shelter, disaster relief assistance, and so on. Typically, their pastor becomes one of the most visible and respected figures in town.

Not all communities of faith, however, are as visible as a stone church building, or even as the blue aluminum building. Remember the sign next to the stone church, the one written in a language that most of us cannot read? It announces that a Korean fellowship meets twice a week in the large congregation's community hall. This community of Christian believers is young, as congregations go. Its membership draws from a growing population of Koreans moving into the area. For some of them, this is their first American experience, having emigrated directly from their homeland. For others, job opportunities have led them from residence in one American city to this one. Often bringing their aging parents and relatives with them, church members in the work force set up households at least three generations deep. The elderly speak virtually no English; those with jobs are learning English or learned it at school in Korea; their school-aged children are balking at having to learn any Korean at all. They think that their grandparents are old-fashioned, embarrassing them by wearing native dress in public. They would rather that church worship were conducted in English, but the elders insist upon Korean. Many of the members hope that the slowly growing congregation can build its own sanctuary building on its own property before they die.

Paying Attention to the Religious Landscape

Our casual drive through town on our way to somewhere else can reveal a lot about religious promise, if we can learn to pay attention. It is not merely that, like the population, religion in

America is becoming more ethnically varied. What about resources for ministry? In such an era of change, what is available
to help congregations reflect upon their life together, to discern
God's calling, and to work through both their strengths and resistances? How can our congregations follow Jesus's admoni-
tion to the twelve to be "wise as serpents and innocent as doves"
(Matthew 10:16)?

In this chapter, I suggest one such tool or model to help with
congregational analysis, strategy, and action.[1] Inherited forms of
thinking and acting—even among institutions—are showing serious signs of wear.[2] Organizational tinkering and adapting is no
longer enough. We need reinventing and transforming! We need
a whole new model. In succeeding chapters, I elaborate upon
each part of this model, drawing on the examples of actual congregations I know.

Foundations: A "Contextual Posture" Grid

How each religious community positions itself depends on both
internal and external issues.[3] Like other organizations today, our
congregations and parishes develop an internal *sense of identity*,
and they also work out a way to *relate to the world* around them.
As these internal and external issues interact with each other, the
four different postures of the grid come to life.

We begin by asking about a church's sense of identity. How
much does the church pay attention primarily to itself? To what
extent and in what ways is it actively concerned for those who
are not part of them? The answers reveal the church's (usually
unspoken) identity bias and show how much it is chiefly *inner-
directed* on the one hand and chiefly *empathetic* on the other.

The church whose Sunday worship service and bulletin includes prayers weekly for elected officials, recent tragedies, and
ongoing issues in the public arena we would understand as being
"empathetic," able to engage genuinely with needs beyond their
walls. By comparison, I used to live a few houses down the street
from a church that had no visibility in the neighborhood other
than that its buildings and parking lot were located there. None

of the church members lived in the neighborhood, not even the pastor. In four years, I heard of them interacting with local residents only once—to ask the homeowners across the street if they would sell their houses to the church. The congregation wanted to tear down the houses to increase the size of its parking lot! Such an interaction suggests a more "inner-directed" congregational attitude, a more inward focus toward its identity—though this should not necessarily be understood as negative or pejorative. At this point, we simply want to recognize the tendency that a church might attend primarily to its own existence and issues. The range between the two identity qualities can be illustrated by a continuum like the one below:

Inner-directed ——————— Empathetic

Next, we consider the world continuum—that is, a church's sense of its "fit" with its world. To what extent does this congregation match its context or express a way of life that mirrors that of its community context? By contrast, to what extent does the parish live in response to a world that it experiences as unfriendly, undesirable, or perhaps hostile? Sometimes groups of believers find themselves living in circumstances that are challenging. Income disparities, racial tensions, and class differences affect churches; these and other daily realities can drive a congregation's specific location on this world axis. In our imaginary road trip, we saw various types of church buildings in different locations of the town. The buildings' styles, as well as their physical location, often symbolize different locations of context, different stances in the world. These differences are the kind that we usually learn as we grow up, using them to separate our world into "us" and "them."

I use the terms *conventionality* and *marginality* to represent the two opposing ends of the "fit" continuum. Conventionality refers to that side of the axis in which the organization or group functions like a hand in a glove within its context. On the other end of this continuum is marginality, which describes a group that is or at least sees itself as being outside of its community's central life.

The story of Samuel the judge reluctantly accepting a request by the elders of Israel to establish a monarchy (1 Samuel 8) illustrates how the poles of this continuum can create group tension. For generations, the Israelites had lived on all sorts of edges. From Abram and Sarai's call to leave their comfortable life and travel for years; to the threatening enmity between the twins Jacob and Esau; to Joseph's rescue of his family; to Moses's "out" and then "in" and then "out" again early years; to the Exodus, the wilderness wanderings, the warfare for the land: Israel was a marginal people!

So when this called community saw a chance to settle down and fit in with neighboring groups, they found it alluring. Usually, there is a sense of high status that accompanies the perception of "arriving," of being like others. No wonder that it felt so desirable to have "a king to govern us, like other nations" (1 Samuel 8:5b; see also 8:20). Forget this marginality business, they might have said; we want to be like everyone else! The range between the two "world fit" qualities can be illustrated by a continuum like the one below:

Conventionality ———————— Marginality

These two continua—"Focus of Identity" and "Stance with World"—form the foundation of our model. By rotating one of the continua to overlay the other, we create a grid with four quadrants. These four quadrants, and how they help us appreciate the opportunities and challenges of ministry in the twenty-first century, are the focus of the rest of the book. This model can help us to discover important things about our churches, for it draws our attention to features of our object of study that we might otherwise miss. Thus, we can view each one of the four quadrants as an "ideal type" of something that never exists so purely in the actual world.[4]

Stance with World

What then are the postures represented in each one of the quadrants? What would a congregation living out of each quadrant look like? In which one is your congregation now? In which do

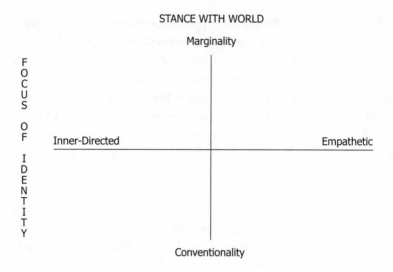

you feel called to become? I begin answering these questions in this chapter and elaborate them throughout the book.

Inner-directed Marginality

One corner of the cultural postures grid describes churches and other religious communities that have been forced by circumstances to live on an edge and spend their main energy taking care of themselves. That is, such congregations more often than not are forced to the margins of their context because of social and economic circumstances. Those who are active in and join this kind of group tend to be functioning in some kind of basic survival mode with life. A significant proportion of the membership often has only a minimal amount of education; they are employed in menial work that is precarious and pays very modestly; they rent or own housing that often is substandard; their overall circumstances combine to deter or limit their ability to improve upon their conditions. Communities in which this kind of church are found usually do not spend a lot of their energy and resources in assisting those from whom this church would draw members. The congregation experiences itself as marginal; it focuses upon providing comfort and hope, doing what it can to support its members. Sometimes, it feels as though the congregation itself is hanging on by the skin of its teeth. Talk of survival is regularly woven into member conversations. These features typify a church that lives out of inner-directed marginality.

Inner-directed marginal congregations and religious groups find strong kinship with their spiritual ancestors in the early chapters of the story of God's chosen people from the Hebrew Bible. Images of the Israelites in the wilderness, free from Egypt but wandering for years, complaining to Moses about their situation, fashioning gods to replace the LORD: such stories become metaphors for the life and temptations of inner-directed marginality. Dreams for security and comfort fill the worship and spiritual life of such religious groups. They are people more of promise than of achievement or arrival.

We often see such an inner-directed marginal church among newly established groups of *immigrants*. Many of the members of these groups find themselves excited about their opportunity but living on the edge of that dream. Their circumstances are tenuous; they need support in order to become oriented to American society, economics, and education. In the cores of our large cities, the classic storefront church also tends to fit into this corner of the grid. *Storefront* churches are often founded by one or two persons with a passionate calling to save residents in destitute surroundings, and a pastor who brings few resources to the task except

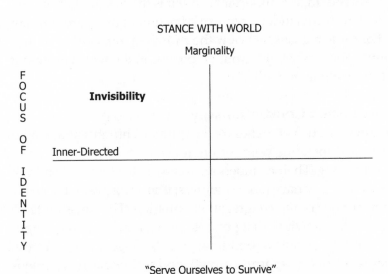

"Serve Ourselves to Survive"
INNER-DIRECTED MARGINALITY

for conviction and commitment of time and energy. They rent or buy abandoned commercial property and provide ministry on the spot. Storefront churches struggle to meet the challenges of survival in the midst of overwhelming odds. Some of these storefront churches are *Pentecostal*. As part of the Protestant Holiness tradition in the United States, Pentecostals have a large urban presence. Their emphasis upon direct experience with the Holy Spirit, confirmed by specific, visible behavior such as speaking in tongues, offers people at the end of their rope a foretaste of God's promises, even in the midst of distress. Although more Pentecostal churches can be found in suburbs today, their origins in struggling city neighborhoods attest to both their marginal and their inner-directed character.

In many respects, living out of this corner of the contextual posture grid is the only choice that many churches, and many new ones, realistically have. For such congregations under imposed stress, living as an ostrich is an appropriate stance to take. Here, the metaphor of the lanky creature with its head in the sand is not out of place. The ostrich is seeking protection from forces of the world that it cannot easily manage. So also do churches in inner-directed marginality find the world around them. Although its stance might appear to outsiders as awkward and self-absorbed, in one important sense it is the best that the church can do. If a church indeed is on an edge, this is the more common one. For these reasons, we view the church in inner-directed marginality as an "invisible" group: typically, in the world around it, it is hardly a player at all.

Inner-directed Conventionality

Sitting next to such churches on the grid are churches that tend to have existed for some years and now see themselves, to some extent, as thriving. Their members are more established economically and socially; they have more resources at their disposal that can be used in service of the congregation's mission. That mission tends to focus upon activities that promote the well-being of the congregation and its members: building projects, Bible studies, retreats and conferences on spiritual growth and wellness, credit unions, etc. Inner-directed conventional religious groups will be more

"Serve Ourselves to Enjoy"
INNER-DIRECTED CONVENTIONALITY

visible in their communities than their marginal counterparts because their overall social circumstances are more parallel to those of their context. Inner-directed conventional religious groups tend to represent stable working-class and middle-class life.

We find such congregations in Scripture too. As we think about our biblical ancestors, we recognize that their focus of identity and stance with the world changed over time. Once the monarchy had been established, and all claims to the throne had been settled,[5] Solomon became king of Israel. Both biblical and archaeological evidence suggest that this era of the monarchy was the most stable and visibly rewarding. God's people now indeed were "like other nations." With such status, of which the LORD had warned Samuel (1 Samuel 8:4-18), came many obligations that the people had to fulfill to the king. Solomon organized the kingdom in a way and to a degree that his father David never did. Taxes, regulations, military conscription, and the like entered Israelite life. For Israel, marginality eventually gave way to conventionality.

Conventionality brings stability to many religious groups today. This quadrant describes churches that have established structures, defined roles, followed procedures and regulations. A settled organization usually feels more as though it fits into the world around it, even when its ideology might critique aspects of that world. For instance, there are religious groups today which espouse a life of being "not of this world," yet their day-to-day operations and economic lifestyle appear virtually indistinguishable from a secular organization. The internal focus of their primary energy—this inner-directedness—helps to validate this kind of church's conventional posture: the end justifies the means.

Of the four locations of contextual posture, the most common one among American religious communities is inner-directed conventionality. Both the drive for stability and the desire to fit into its world are strong features of human nature, especially in its collective forms. So, where might we discover demographic patterns that implicitly encourage inner-directed conventionality? Typically in suburban communities. This trend is not new; Gibson Winter identified and critiqued it four decades ago.[6] He pointed out that, by the mid-twentieth century, Protestant denominations had shifted from inner cities to suburbs. This shift led to a focus on local congregations as middle class, whose "association by likeness"[7] disconnected them from the complex interdependence that exists in a metropolitan area. Winter claimed that this new focus resulted in Protestant conformity to economic standards, especially in attracting middle-class people to congregations located in residential communities.[8] Today, well-established and relatively stable towns and cities with significant middle-class populations also will reveal a noticeable share of religious groups typified by their inner-directed conventionality.

I don't mean to assess this specific contextual posture negatively. One of the aspects of this model that makes it so interesting is that every part of this grid contains features that can function in ministry either as strengths or as hindrances. Being inner-directed can function as a survival focus for building the church's faith; conventionality can provide an avenue of accomplishment, confidence, and access to resources. And yet I am concerned about the overabundance of congregations in inner-directed conventionality.

The danger of this posture is that it can act like an ostrich when it already appears to have some lemonade stands. Its signs of stability are usually interpreted (implicitly) as indications of the congregation's earlier success at making lemonade—i.e., overcoming difficult circumstances by creating something positive out of them. A church's very own accomplishments therefore can end up creating a false sense of security. If the congregation believes, as it is tempted to do in inner-directed conventionality, that "we can survive anything now," it will tend to ignore new lemons that come its way. It might not feel the need to stick its head in the sand, since it has what it believes are functional lemonades stands, behind which it now hides. On the other hand, if a church in this posture finds a way to pick up the new lemons, it begins a journey toward the next posture, toward new possibilities and growth.

Empathetic Conventionality

There are many biblical texts in both the Hebrew and Christian Bibles that admonish the believing community to think and act outside of itself. We hear their stirring ring in such texts as "You shall love the alien as yourself" (Lev. 19:34b) and "learn to do good; seek justice, rescue the oppressed, defend the orphan, plead for the widow" (Isa. 1:17). This tradition might seem to play only a minor part in Hebrew religious thought, but it becomes echoed later in the words of Jesus and Paul:

> "Love your enemies and pray for those who persecute you" (Matt. 5:44)
> "In everything do to others as you would have them do to you; for this is the law and the prophets" (Matt. 7:12)
> "Bear one another's burdens, and in this way you will fulfill the law of Christ" (Gal. 6:2)
> "Let each of you look not to your own interests, but to the interests of others" (Phil. 2:4)

While we rarely refute the validity of these claims upon the faithful, we also don't always act upon them, do we? Yet there seem to be some religious groups for whom this call to empathy is an absolute core of their life together. You and I know churches that do not shy away from actively engaging needs in the

STANCE WITH WORLD

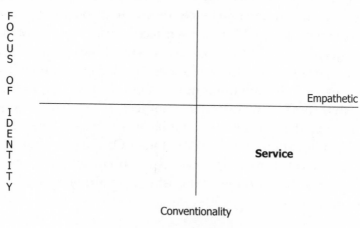

F
O
C
U
S

O
F

I
D
E
N
T
I
T
Y

Empathetic

Service

Conventionality

"Serve Others with Our Abundance"
EMPATHETIC CONVENTIONALITY

wider world. These are congregations that promote action and discussion about how to help others, particularly those whose worldly conditions are distressing in one way or another. These are "empathetic" communities of faith, ones that put a notice-able amount of their resources into meeting need somewhere in the public arena.

In the last generation or so, forms of church empathy have included running soup kitchens and clothes closets, tutoring at schools with low test scores, mentoring troubled teens, helping to build and operate retirement homes, maintaining a substantial percentage of the annual budget for various mission programs, and the like. These are services to the community, compelled at least initially by a clear sense of religious duty toward the pub-lic arena. What makes this contextual posture a conventional one is the high comfort level that the congregation has with its own community, with its practices and values. Typically, empa-thetic conventional churches consist of members with substantial resources—education, employment, experiences, skills, net-works, and so on—even though they do not necessarily repre-sent the city's or town's upper echelons. This kind of church's empathy is directed toward those who exist in a recognizably less privileged part of society. The congregation serves "the needy," "the poor," "the underprivileged," and other such segments of the population that rarely would be members of their church.

While some conventional congregations are able to undertake this fundamental shift from inner-directedness to empathy, such a shift has not been all that common. When it does occur, empathetic conventionality is most likely to be found in urban areas. There, long-standing congregations who have grappled with dramatic and repeated changes in their city's core sometimes eventually decide that God is calling them to more challenging forms of ministry right where they are. Suburbs and stand-alone towns are less likely to produce churches in this contextual posture, since they typically do not undergo the degree or complexity of change in population, ethnicity, economy, lifestyle and such that occur in major metropolitan areas. Thus, even though this move is possible and has been made, it is not widespread.

Why is this the case? It is here that the model reminds us of how strong the pull is toward conventionality and comfort. It takes less collective energy to attend to the concerns and needs of the people in your own church than to those of people outside of your church. Gibson Winter's critique of suburban church life needs to be understood in a demographic context. If inner cities have more of all kinds of distresses and challenges, suburban churches appear to have created their own ostrich holes of security. They leave the lemons alone. However, churches living out of the empathetic conventional quadrant acknowledge that the lemons are there. These congregations have found a way to overcome their inner inertia and respond with some heart, in specific ways, to the biblical witness for "the other."

Empathetic Marginality

Empathy in action is easier for a church to embrace out of the conventional stance—but it is not the only way. The other way to be empathetic is the harder one, the road less traveled, a way of Christian witness that seems to redefine the enterprise. The contextual posture of "empathetic marginality" is not prevalent. It seems to occur at any given time in only a small percentage of religious communities. Being empathetically marginal is difficult to attain and difficult to maintain; this makes it the most demanding of the four postures on this grid. For some religious groups, it also will be unpopular, seen as somehow not quite orthodox. Yet we will see later in the book why it is precisely the posture of empathetic marginality with which many congregations in our new century need to grapple. It is also the case that illustrating what an empathetic marginal church looks like can be trickier than it sounds.

What distinguishes any religious group living out of empathetic marginality is the way in which it uses its self-understanding of "being different" as a spiritual and strategic impetus for ministry. This means that the congregation in question does not allow its condition of "being on the edge" to limit or stifle its capacity for genuine interest and action on behalf of others. Such churches are neither self-absorbed nor self-pitying but draw instead upon a hard-won, deep theological understanding of what impels them to do ministry. It is necessary to make the same point coming from the other direction of the grid. An empathetically marginal church is willing and able to direct its compassion for those beyond its doors in ways that challenge the community's status quo and call for the church to struggle in its relationship with society.

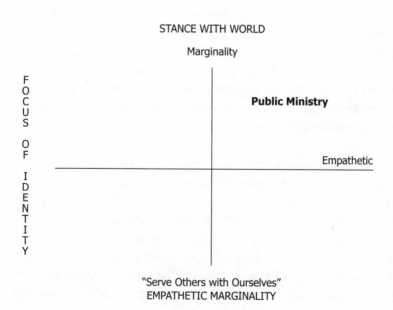

STANCE WITH WORLD

Marginality

F
O
C
U
S

O
F

I
D
E
N
T
I
T
Y

Public Ministry

Empathetic

"Serve Others with Ourselves"
EMPATHETIC MARGINALITY

This description of empathetic marginality reminds us of the scriptural prophetic tradition, but I want you to think first beyond these familiar, although admittedly uncomfortable, religious categories. Where in the Bible do we hear ourselves called to a ministry of marginal empathy? Christians recognize in Jesus's use of "love your neighbor as yourself" (Mark 12:31) a reference to a key religious obligation in the ancient Levitical code. Amidst the many statements there about sexual relations and ritual purity, we also find exhortations such as "You shall not defraud your neighbor" (Lev. 19:13a), "You shall not render an unjust judgment" (Lev. 19:15a), and the verse that Jesus cited, "You shall not take vengeance or bear a grudge against any of your people, but you shall love your neighbor as yourself: I am the LORD" (Lev. 19-18). It is common simply to hear these exhortations as laws or rules of love by which believers are called to live. In such an interpretive context, the empathy indeed is highlighted. But we find the driving force for it in particular biblical texts, such as in Leviticus and Deuteronomy. In these several passages, the texts tie empathetic behavior to the chosen people's own history of marginality:

> When an alien resides with you in your land, you shall not oppress the alien. The alien who resides with you shall be to you as the citizen among you; you shall love the alien as yourself, *for you were aliens in the land of Egypt:* I am the LORD. (Lev. 19:33–34, italics mine)

As we know, "the land of Egypt" represents Israel's life of slavery to the Pharoah, one of the chosen people's most dramatic experiences of marginality in every possible way. This tie made between Israel's own historical experience and God's call to care for others is echoed and elaborated in Deuteronomy. In one passage, the LORD speaks in terms of both praise and justice, and the range of God's care includes two more categories of persons with a fragile social existence:

> For the LORD your God is God of gods and Lord of lords, the great God, mighty and awesome, who is not partial and takes no bribe, who executes justice for the orphan and the widow, and who loves the strangers, providing them food and clothing. You shall also love

the stranger, *for you were strangers in the land of Egypt.* (Deut. 10:17-19,
   italics mine)

Again, the exhortation to demonstrate active concern for those
who are not part of Israel (empathy) is justified by a key reference to Israel's own history (marginality).

Themes of justice make a strong case in the prophetic literature. Specific references to these three categories—widows, orphans, and aliens/strangers—are found in Isaiah 1:17, Zechariah
7:10, Malachi 3:5, and Ezekiel 22:7. One implication of these and
other texts is that justice for those on the fringes moves beyond
matters of welfare alone. Furthermore, Amos's most famous po-
etic call connects public acts of good with a life of faith defined
not merely by religious activities: "But let justice roll down like
waters, and righteousness like an ever-flowing stream" (Amos
5:24). We are all too aware of how, in our day, Christians often
treat righteous living as something personal, something that
can be carried out without any reference to community well-
being. I am proposing that "empathetic marginality" is one po-
tent way by which today's churches might consider their challenge to ministry in the future.

Yet empathetically marginal religious bodies are hard to find.
In American history, they might be most easily spotted through
the activities of such groups as Friends' meetings (Quakers), for
instance. As a historic peace church, the Friends oppose war and
were among the first to free their own slaves and oppose slavery.[9]
Any group of believers that makes a conscious decision to behave in a certain way, in order to meet the needs of another seg-
ment of society—even if that behavior will put it at odds with its
society—is acting out of empathetic marginality. For this reason,
in our day and time, the few communities of faith who live out
of this corner of the grid likely will be found in metropolitan areas. It is in an expanding and sometimes rapidly changing demographic context that opportunities for empathy with marginality
are most likely.

Facing such circumstances, churches aspiring to grow in their
faithfulness might find a telling metaphor in the ancient story of
Jacob wrestling with the angel (Gen. 32:22-31). After years of ab-

sence from his estranged brother, Esau, Jacob prepares to appease the one whom he tricked out of his birthright. He sends a very large offering of fine animals (remember, theirs was a nomadic lifestyle) with instructions to his servants of what to say once they meet Esau. Jacob then sends his family and the rest of the party on ahead and spends the night alone. We all have puzzled over this strange episode, of the man who wrestles with Jacob, putting the future patriarch's hip out of joint but also blessing him and bestowing upon him a new name ("Israel—the one who strives with God"). Israel recognizes the divine presence in his experience and acknowledges it as he names the spot. He leaves the next morning, limping but headed for a meeting with his brother, for whom "to see your face is like seeing the face of God" (Gen. 33:10c).

Through his night of divine struggle, Jacob receives a fresh mission, but he is marked for life with an injury that cannot heal. That injury becomes a symbol of marginalization. Churches who can accept their own night of wrestling with God stand a chance of finding where their own injury, their weakness, their marginality rests. It is only as a community of faith accepts its own particular form of being limp in God's name that it can become a witness out of both marginality and empathy. In the last two chapters, we will hear about two particular congregations that I think have had their wrestling matches with God and found ways to receive their limp along with their name.

General Observations

Reading over the brief descriptions of each posture begs for clarification: Why, for example, are American churches found across the grid in the manner described here? Why are some postures "better" or "worse" than others (i.e., descriptive analysis vs. normative judgment)? And what happens on the grid to congregations over time?

American religious groups nowadays—and especially Christian churches—are distributed across the grid something like this:

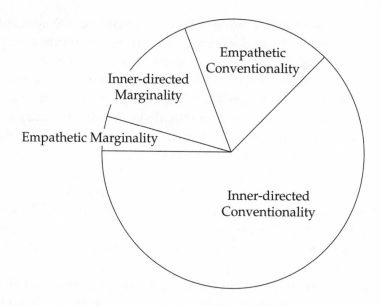

I draw these conclusions based on my pastoral experience coupled with graduate study and research, seminary teaching, and church training leadership. Of the estimated 350,000 houses of worship in the United States, a large majority has existed for many years, but growing numbers of churches are a generation or less in age. The dynamics of change since World War II have led to massive efforts among many churches aimed at survival and repetition, rather than adaptation or transformation. This is one main reason why inner-directed conventionality is so dominant right now. However, the seeds for a new configuration of distribution across the grid continue to be sown in society. It remains to be seen how that configuration could look—and I hazard some guesses in the final chapter.

Second, a look at distribution across the grid also points to how internal and external factors affecting today's faith communities can be very subtle. The more dramatic factors, the easily visible ones, often deal with race, economy, and social class. Yet even what appears to be stable can mislead; consider how the parents of Baby Boomers assumed that their children would return to church once they married and began raising children. The "return rate" was much lower than the parents imagined.[10]

The more subtle factors of change deal often with the congregation's internal attitudes of complacence or unwillingness to try new things. Members of well-established congregations will drive back to their familiar church building for years after moving away from the neighborhood that is changing. Rather than figure out how to serve the new residents, congregations have tended to keep things as they "always have been"—a sure way to hasten an eventual demise.

Third, in the matter of the relative strength or "purity" of the postures, the grid is not lock-step or necessarily absolute. That is, it is possible to observe congregations that are less or more purely in one or another posture, as well as others that are closer or farther away from the boundaries of other postures. Church A's attitudes and behavior might be predictable, repetitious, and inwardly focused, as it has been for several years. This pattern would place it squarely in the middle of the inner-directed conventional posture. On the other hand, Church C might appear to be very similar to Church A, but it might have begun to cooperate with Church B on a homeless feeding ministry. Not too many of the members of Church C participate, but they are committed to the work. Church B has led its town in a feeding program for years and also runs a clothes closet, hosts an ecumenical Thanksgiving Service, and financially supports a job training center. Church D is eight years old and its members bring their families and friends to the training center and the clothing bank; their pastor works full-time as a mail carrier and is invited every year to participate in the thanksgiving service.

As the diagram on the next page shows, congregations will find themselves more or less in one contextual posture or another.

Fourth, congregations do change postures over time. Religious communities that initially just survive for a number of years often move into a conventional posture (or from one conventional posture to another) and remain there for a long time. It is common for them to begin in inner-directed marginality, especially if their primary clientele is an immigrant or other socially "at-risk" population. How many times might one particular church move over its lifetime? One move (two postures) is

STANCE WITH WORLD

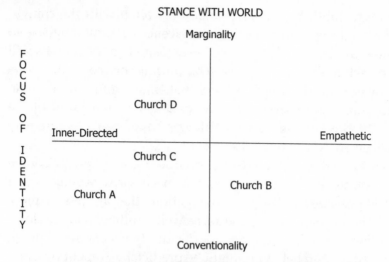

RELATIVE STRENGTH WITHIN A POSTURE: A SAMPLE
The closer the congregation is to another boundary, the more capable it is of
eventually moving into the posture on the other side of that boundary.

typical; two moves (three postures) are possible but less likely. This is because the postures represent significant elements of the church's culture, and culture does not change quickly or easily. I have written on church culture extensively elsewhere.[11]

What might these moves look like within the grid? The most common posture change is from inner-directed marginality (a fragile organizational condition) to inner-directed conventionality (stable but inwardly focused). Here, survival seems assured, but the ability to interpret the congregation's context in light of its calling has not been nurtured. The second most likely move would occur within the conventional half of the grid, from inner-directedness to empathy. This move represents a wider reach in the congregation's sense of ministry, but without rocking the boat of the church's sense of fitting into its community. Not every church that reaches conventionality moves into empathy. The least likely move, as I have noted already, is into empathetic marginality. This corner of the grid can be reached from two different directions, depending on the congregation's recognized social location at the time of its founding. For example, ethnic churches would enter empathetic marginality out of a history of socially forced marginality, while majority (i.e., of European descent) churches would be more likely to enter out of a history of conventional experience with its community. These patterns of movement will be part of the discussion in the upcoming chapters, as we look at case churches.

Finally, there remains the question of whether this grid implies a judgment of better or worse postures. Is inner-directed marginality "bad" in itself, while empathetic marginality is the noble goal? To answer these questions with a simple "yes" or "no" would mislead the reader and oversimplify the dynamics that the grid seeks to illuminate. At one level, these categories are descriptive: they explain things as they occur. At another level, the grid can function to assess the integrity of a church's theology with its practice. It is not my purpose to shame any congregation or to affix negative labels. At the same time, the grid does suggest how potential for various forms of ministry will be more or less likely, depending upon where any religious group finds itself on the grid. These likely ministry differences between postures will be illustrated in the following chapters.

Broaching the matter of theology suggests a corollary question about ideological perspective. I do not conceive of this contextual posture grid of congregations in terms of any one brand of theology. Churches probably will continue to be spread across the grid in every imaginable theological stripe. Yet I also do not think that it is necessarily possible to move into empathetic marginality by theologizing "any old which way." By the end of the book, I hope that readers will consider that the challenges posed by empathetic marginality will end up debunking any facile theology or spiritual comfort zone. As Alfred North Whitehead once wrote, "The pure conservative is fighting against the essence of the universe."[12] Whatever a congregation might be trying to preserve for posterity will be tested by the kind of spiritual honesty that empathetic marginality requires. If we are people who believe deeply that God seeks to "do a new thing" (Rev.21:5), then our imaginations must be ready for the forms our empathy and our marginality might take.

From here, it will be more useful to elaborate upon each one of the contextual postures through illustrations from actual congregations. Specific stories will demonstrate what the grid reveals about church life and what else we might learn from this model. To these and related tasks we now turn.

Notes

1. This resource does not reflect the conclusions of a single research project or source of information. Instead, it is a model born out of decades of my reflection on American congregations—as a pastor, as one observing churches and pastors, in my graduate study of sociology and organizational theory, and in years of teaching hundreds of theological students. Models always are limited in scope and application, but that should not prevent their being developed, applied, and modified.

2. See George B. Thompson, Jr., *Treasures in Clay Jars: New Ways to Understand Your Church* (Cleveland: The Pilgrim Press, 2003), ch. 1, "Horseless Carriage: Why Another 'New' Paradigm?"

3. Internal and external matters are common categories of discussion in organizational theory. See, for instance, Edgar Schein, *Organizational Culture and Leadership*, 3d ed. (San Francisco: Jossey-Bass, 2004), ch. 5, "Assumptions About External Adaptation Issues," and ch. 6, "Assumptions about Managing Internal Integration."

4. The notion of "ideal types" was introduced by the great social scientist Max Weber; see its discussion in Julien Freund, *The Sociology of Max Weber,* translated by Mary Ilford, (New York: Vintage Books, 1969), 59–71, esp. 66.

5. A religious community's transitions from the inner-directed marginal posture to a conventional posture can be rocky, as the story of the early Israelite monarchy suggests. The closing chapters of 2 Samuel (13-21) and the opening chapter of 1 Kings display a lot of stealth and violence in a period of change. Several characters sought to gain control as the Israelites moved out of rule by judges and into their hoped-for stability and status with a monarchy. Certainly we do not expect actual warfare and murder when our congregations experience major change! And yet, we know that churches do become conflicted at times; sometimes this conflict occurs as churches move out of one contextual posture and into another one.

6. Gibson Winter, *The Suburban Captivity of the Churches: An Analysis of Protestant Responsibility in the Expanding Metropolis* (New York: Macmillan, 1962); see esp. ch. 1, 2, and 3.

7. Ibid., 74.

8. Ibid., 76-77.

9. Summaries of the history and ministry of the Society of Friends are easily found on the following websites (accessed 26 December 2006): www.religiousmovements.lib.virginia.edu/nrms/quak.html and www.religioustolerance.org/quaker.htm

10. For a discussion of research on Baby Boomers and their church involvement, see Wade Clark Roof, *A Generation of Seekers: The Spiritual Journeys of the Baby Boom Generation* (New York: HarperSanFrancisco, 1994), esp. ch. 2 on influences from the cultural revolution of the 1960s, and ch. 6, analyzing trends of Boomer religious participation.

11. See especially George B. Thompson, Jr., "Leadership for Congregational Vitality: Paradigmatic Explorations in Open Systems Organizational Culture Theory," *Journal of Religious Leadership,* vol. 2, no. 1, Spring 2003, 53-86, available on www.arl-jrl.org; see also my *How to Get Along with Your Pastor: Creating Partnership for Doing Ministry* (Cleveland: The Pilgrim Press, 2006), Part I.

12. Alfred North Whitehead, *Adventures of Ideas* (New York: The Free Press, 1933), 274.

CHAPTER 3

Edge of Nowhere

The More Common Edge

INNER-DIRECTED MARGINALITY

Cities: Promise with Peril

Chicago is a big city. For much of the twentieth century, Chicago maintained the distinction of being the second largest city in the United States, second only to New York. Sprawling as it did late in the nineteenth century away from the western shores of Lake Michigan, Chicago began humbly, as most cities do. From trading post to port to immigration destination to burnt-out devastation to world-class architecture to gangster hub to sports mecca to international panache, Chicago has a history that reveals much of the story of the United States. Yet, if you want to understand Chicago, you have to take into account not just the breathtaking skyline and the parks, but Back of the Yards, Chinatown, Gresham, Cabrini Green, Pilsen, Woodlawn, Mount Greenwood, Rogers Park, and many other distinctive neighborhoods as well.

Visiting a big city like Chicago offers a vivid lesson in society, economics and culture, all rolled into one. Streets and blocks on the "North Side" where Germans and Swedes first settled, now bustle with people of darker skin, whose languages are not familiar to Europeans. New restaurants emit scents that tantalize old residents with their exotic ambience. On the "South Side," whites in the 1960s moved out of many neighborhoods very quickly, as civil rights efforts broke real estate "redlining." African Americans moved in—and they stayed. Many South Side neighborhoods remain heavily African American, a number of them boasting attractive brick homes with manicured lawns and many churches.

Chicago's history of growth and prosperity, however, is not all rosy. Following the Great Fire of 1871 were stark and harsh stories of struggle, danger, poverty, and indifference. It was to just such difficult conditions that Jane Addams, the founder of Hull House—a "settlement" for immigrants—devoted her energy and resources in Chicago for more than four decades over the turn of the twentieth century. In 1892, as she opened Hull House's doors, not too far southwest of the downtown Loop, Addams described the neighborhood in these words:

> Between Halsted Street and the river live about ten thousand Italians: Neapolitans, Silicians, and Calabrians, with an occasional Lombard or Venetian. To the south on Twelfth Street are many Germans, and side streets are given over almost entirely to Polish and Russian Jews. Still further south, these Jewish colonies merge into a huge Bohemian colony, so vast that Chicago ranks as the third Bohemian city in the world. To the northwest are many Canadian-French, clannish in spite of their long residence in America, and to the north are many Irish and first-generation Americans. On the streets directly west and farther north are well-to-do English-speaking families, many of whom own their houses and have lived in the neighborhood for years. I know one man who is still living in his old farm-house. This corner of Polk and Halsted Streets is in the fourteenth precinct of the nineteenth ward. This ward has a population of about fifty thousand, and at the last presidential election registered 7072 voters. . . . The streets are inexpressibly dirty, the number of schools inadequate, factory legislation unenforced, the street-lighting bad, the paving miserable and altogether lacking in the alleys and small streets, and the stables defy all laws of sanitation. Hundred of homes are unconnected with the street sewer. . . . An unscrupulous contractor regards no basement as too dark, no stable loft too foul, no rear shanty too provisional, no tenement room too small for his workroom, as these conditions imply low rental.[1]

More than a century later, Addams's detailed description sounds familiar in a new way. In many urban neighborhoods, one ethnic group or another dominates, even if today they are from other continents than Europe. Although civil rights issues do receive more attention than they used to, not everyone who lives in the United States benefits in equal measure from its espoused freedom and opportunity. This is especially true for people who arrive here with not much more than the clothes on their backs. They are often rudely thrust into a world in which the glitter and glamour is visible but far out of their reach.

A Checkerboard of Fragility

What does a general social analysis of immigrant city life, then and now, do to help us understand American churches? It reminds us that all churches emerge and exist within a particular context. The people who live in the vicinity of your church building, what they do, what they like, what resources and connections they have, what jobs are available to them—these and other factors have some significant bearing on your church's life and opportunities.

Our discussion about Chicago helps us to see something else, too. Jane Addams' summary of the nineteenth ward in 1892 ends on a stark note. The place that she chose to call home, the place that she chose to do ministry, was home to an overwhelming variety of peoples. Some of them were forced by circumstances beyond their control to live in conditions that were difficult, dreary, and dangerous. Immigrant life, yesterday and today, often puts people on a fragile edge. Addams gave her life to helping people in these conditions pursue a better life. Even though her efforts eventually became recognized nationally and around the world (she was one of two recipients of the Nobel Peace Prize in 1930[2]), Chicago—like cities of all sizes—continues to have neighborhoods where residents struggle mightily.

Decades after Addams's death, my own experiences in Chicago led me to ponder many of the same issues. For five years, I worked in Hyde Park on Chicago's South Side and lived nine miles away, in another Chicago neighborhood. Hyde Park is home to the world–renowned University of Chicago and the

Museum of Science and Industry, just across Lake Shore Drive from Lake Michigan itself.

Driving to and from Hyde Park, it was very obvious to me that many areas on the South Side still were quite barren and bleak. One of the routes that I traveled runs west out of Hyde Park onto Garfield Avenue, over the Dan Ryan expressway to Ashland Avenue, then south five miles to 95th Street. Block by block, that stretch down Ashland contained a dizzying mixture of dug-in destitution and stabs at hope. Many of the old brick buildings were abandoned or sported hand-painted signs announcing the name of a church, its pastor, and a weekly schedule of activities. It finally occurred to me that there were quite a few churches in that five-mile stretch. So, one day, I counted all of the church signs that I could see from the street, on Ashland Avenue between Garfield and 95th Street. The total? Forty-eight signs. In a forty-block section of a major street on Chicago's South Side, cutting through neighborhoods in which poverty was more common than automatic dishwashers, there was more than one church per block!

With few exceptions, all of these churches easily could be located on our grid of contextual postures in the inner-directed marginality quadrant. This is the quadrant in which the churches

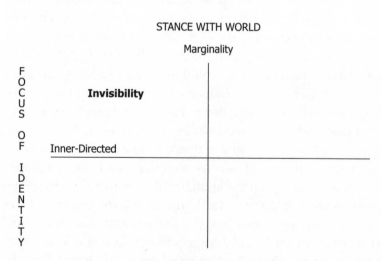

STANCE WITH WORLD

Marginality

F
O
C   **Invisibility**
U
S

O
F   Inner-Directed

I
D
E
N
T
I
T
Y

"Serve Ourselves to Survive"
CHURCH ON THE EDGE OF NOWHERE

are, for all intents and purposes, invisible to society. These congregations serve a clientele that teeters on an edge—often the edge of America's socioeconomic system. The ethnic groups that surrounded Hull House at the turn of the twentieth century were just such a clientele. New arrivals, with few material resources and skills, like most immigrant groups throughout American history were valued for cheap labor and not much else. Freed African American slaves faced similar circumstances, without the advantage eventually of being able to visually blend into society, once one had learned how to "fit in." Churches in inner-directed marginality know that their members, and their mission field, somehow do not fit in. In all factors that make a difference in the world, these congregations serve on "the edge of nowhere."

Biblical Echoes

We do not have to read very far into the Bible to notice how life in inner-directed marginal churches reflects part of the story line of our spiritual ancestors. For the people who founded many American immigrant congregations, life had been good once, back in their homeland. Immigrant communities have something in common with the patriarch Jacob and his family who, although living nomadically, had created a comfortable life. The dramatic and theologically inspiring story of Jacob's favored son Joseph (Genesis 37–50) traces the family's life from one of plenty to famine to rescue and relief in Egypt. Their status as favored immigrants in the land of Pharoah turned sour after Joseph's death, when they were forced to work construction for a new Pharoah's many building projects (Exodus 1:8–14). Moses's intervention on his own people's behalf led to the wonder-filled escape from Egypt, the Passover, but then to years of wandering, worrying, and complaining (Exodus 15:22ff.). Along the way, their great leader Moses died and was replaced by Joshua, who led them eventually, through battle, into settlement of a land that the Israelites could call their own (see the book of Joshua).

This story line, which begins with Abram and Sarai (Genesis 12ff.) and continues all the way through Joshua's leadership and death, tells of generations of God's people living on edges. The elderly couple leaving home and traveling until their deaths; the son born of an outlandish promise, after his parents already took matters into their own hands; the twin son who tricks his father out of the other son's inheritance and spends much of his life on the run; the favored son whose brothers get jealous and sell him to a caravan, then tell their father that he is dead; the prisoner who wins Pharoah's favor and becomes Egypt's second in command; the governor who uses stealth and deception to save his family from a famine; the oppressed brick makers who flee with their families out of Egypt under cover of darkness and are saved from certain slaughter through direct divine intervention: such stories go on and on in the early books of the Hebrew Bible. They are not stories of comfort and security but of uncertainty, threat, ill will, subjugation, and survival.

Throughout the centuries of Christianity in America, not every congregation that has been founded here began under such conditions. We will consider these more favored churches in the next chapter. It is clear, however, in surveying American history, that many local communities of faith were established in spite of their arduous circumstances. The description of Jane Addams's Chicago at the beginning of this chapter provides one snapshot of such circumstances. Even more dramatically, African American slaves—and later, freed slaves—gathered regularly and often secretly under brush arbors to affirm their trust in a God who sets people free, just as with the Israelites under Pharoah. For a torn and constantly disrupted community to believe that God loved and cared for them, in spite of what they endured daily, is an astounding testament to their faith.[3] In these and other distressed communities, living as an ostrich is usually the only way to affirm dignity and preserve integrity.

Characteristics

In other words, these kinds of communities create churches that are both inner-directed and marginal. They typically are congregations still in their first generation or so of existence. That is, the congregation draws from a cohort in the population that itself is marginal in society, especially in terms of economic well-being, social status, and political influence. This marginality is most intense during the early decades of a group's presence in the country. In many cases, it has been racially motivated, as the history of African Americans continues to remind us, but not exclusively so. Ethnic groups from European countries have been treated marginally and cruelly in the United States as well.[4] What are common among both racial and ethnic churches, however, are the contours of their social status and their understandable and legitimate preoccupation. They exist on an edge of society that others do not deliberately seek, and thus they concentrate upon affirming dignity for their people when no other institution will do so.

So how might we summarize the general characteristics of the churches in this quadrant? Such churches in inner-directed marginality tend not to be long-standing institutions but rather exist on the newer side of the organizational lifecycle.[5] This condition reflects many of its other characteristics. Congregants are very aware of their "edge" status, often through limited employment opportunities affected in part by language and education. The congregation is highly inner-focused; needs of parishioners tend to be greater on any given day than the available resources, so meeting those needs becomes a top priority. This focus means that the congregation casts a fairly small net: its circle of potential and actual participants is often clearly understood by race, ethnicity, or socioeconomic condition. Since these conditions typically are undervalued by the wider society, this congregation also serves to affirm that community's cultural qualities and distinctiveness. If the congregation is evangelical by nature—and many of them are—its net is cast into that part of its community where it expects to meet others like them with great need. Services provided are foundational, from invitations to salvation, to prayer partners and Bible study groups, to a place to stay, to help looking for a job, and so on.

But these easily observable features of an inner-directed marginal congregation do not tell its whole story as you will know from similar churches in your own neighborhood. We only fully appreciate its ethos if we also listen to what is publicly affirmed. Consider many African American churches that either have been or continue to live in this quadrant: Perhaps you've heard said during worship things like:

- "God makes a way out of no way."
- "There are no little 'U's or big 'I's in this church."
- "We've come this far by faith."

The first and third of these sayings emphasize an historic conviction that, in spite of the atrocities of slavery and segregation, believers trust that God continues to act on their behalf. The second saying emphasizes that each member of the congregation is important because of their status as one of God's precious children. To speak such is to counterbalance messages heard and acted out from the larger society, messages that degrade both the individual and the gathered community. Sayings like these serve to affirm and clarify the values that the congregation seeks to live out in all that it does.

Even more deeply than these types of sayings, however, rest the inner-directed marginal church's most basic assumptions.[6] Because these beliefs are taken for granted, they are rarely in awareness and thus even more rarely spoken. Yet their power in the congregation is inescapable. For instance, we could anticipate that churches in inner-directed marginality would believe deep down that "the world is not safe or friendly." Because of their social and economic conditions, such a church also might believe deep down that "people who are not like us do not have our best interests in mind." Sometimes these deeply held beliefs lead to church behavior that could contradict something that is affirmed aloud. Such contradictions can and do occur in other quadrants of the contextual posture grid as well.[7]

Because the persons who inhabit these churches bear almost no economic influence or social capital, society tends to ignore them. They do not count for much. Their virtually forced preoccupation with their congregations' own identities and interests is not to be judged or condemned; indeed, at this point, it is necessary. A church in inner-directed marginality lives as a seemingly invisible community, on the edge of nowhere. It is typically just getting by.

Where in your community would you find such a congregation? Who are the people who populate it? What are their lives like?

Down but Not Out

"Getting by" is a real honest-to-goodness strength in such churches, not something to disdain or demean. It is very important for those of us who have had no direct experience with inner-directed marginality to appreciate its origins and its character—for its own sake and for ours. Because American society continues to remain relatively fluid, this kind of church will continue to emerge and exist. Such new inner-directed marginal congregations will be dominated by the skin tones of whatever ethnic groups dominate American immigration. For the foreseeable future, these tones will be brown (Hispanic) and yellow (Asian). This projection alone is cause for the white majority of American Christians to think about their faith and its witness in fresh ways.

Inner-directed marginality is not bad in itself. It exists in large part due to wide-ranging factors, to which the responses that create inner-directed marginality make sense. There is a time in the early years of many congregations when this posture serves its people well. Our purpose is not to disdain such congregations but to understand and appreciate them.

The stark challenges of such inner-directed marginal churches call for a certain kind of leadership. Their pastors especially must be people who can both nurture and inspire. Sometimes, just getting by is all that the member or congregation can expect, and the pastor must embody this strength. She or he often is only one or two steps ahead of many congregants: the pastor typically works a full-time job with salary and benefits in order to make possible the time and resources directed for the church. As Massey and McKinney point out, the pastor of an urban African American church typically fulfills many roles. Especially as persons and families relocated to the North for increased economic and social opportunities, the pastor would be called on to help locate housing and jobs, to advocate for and speak on behalf of equal treatment and opportunity, to assist in financial crises, to advise, counsel, and so on.[8] An inner-directed marginal church is challenged daily to match needs with resources. Members look to their pastor for ways to bring any and all such resources into reach. To lead here is to be like Moses (perhaps with those moments of complaining to God included!).

"Like the Nations"

A church that begins its existence as inner-directed and marginal could spend many years in this quadrant. Yet, life does not stand still. It might be possible to imagine a congregation that remains there indefinitely, although the organizational drive for stability usually leads to a change on the grid. What conditions and circumstances contribute to this shift? What does it take for an inner-directed marginal church to move into another quadrant on the contextual posture grid? When is it able to move into that quadrant?

The following story helps to answer these questions. When I was growing up, there was an Assembly of God church on the other side of town, in a neighborhood with mill workers and mechanics living with their families in small houses. Their cars were faded and sometimes rusty, and more than one yard had tall weeds growing up around a pickup on blocks. The few boys from that congregation with whom I was acquainted wore blue jeans and plaid flannel shirts to school. I didn't know anything about the church itself, except that it seemed strange.

Two decades later, the sons of the farmer who had owned all the fields around my parents' house decided to sell off part of the parcel to the west. The old, rickety wood house that had sat on one corner of the parcel had burned down. Five acres went up for sale, and the buyer was none other than the Assembly of God church from across town. It then built one of those single-story, round sanctuary structures and brought in gravel for parking. As the years went by, the church added a couple of wings to its sanctuary; it paved over an acre of its parking area; it bought the rest of the farmer's land that was available back to the railroad tracks; and it changed the church's name. Now it is called a "Life Center"—with "of the Assemblies of God" written in much smaller print on its street sign. The cars parked in that lot now are shiny. On summer evenings, when I was visiting my father, I could hear from across the parking lot electric guitar music that I would classify as soft rock. Very few senior citizens attend this "life center;" it appears on Sunday mornings and Sunday evenings to be filled with younger Baby Boomers and Generation X folks.

What has happened to this congregation in the years since I was young? How did it transform itself from a struggling, working-class church on one end of town to a contemporary, seemingly middle-class, resourceful congregation located prominently on a road leading out the other end of town? What lemons did it find with which to make such lemonade?

Eventually, it seems, most inner-directed marginal churches either close down or move out of their marginality. As time goes by, conditions and opportunities tend to improve for those segments of the American population that would be most likely to join inner-directed marginal churches. These improvements have been especially true since World War II, in economic and educational terms as well as in general social change. The social power of what some scholars refer to as "Protestant aristocracy and caste" in the United States[9] has all but eroded. All of these general observations help us to understand how churches like the Assembly of God in my home town could change in its stance toward the world. No longer are they as likely to meet the world around them as disinterested or hostile. For those congregations who lived out of the inner-directed marginal grid in days gone by, their clientele "fits in" better now. The world is less an adversary or oppressor than it used to be.

I suggest that the most likely contextual posture move for inner-directed marginal churches is away from the marginality and into conventionality. Having endured many social and economic tests, the membership in many respects has found its way into sharing part of the American Dream. It is this quality that makes them conventional—in one important sense, like every-one else. They no longer live as though on an edge; our human need for some level of comfort and acceptance tends to keep us away from edges from which we have managed to flee.

So, where are these churches now? What is their new under-standing of identity? How do they relate with each other (which also means potential new members) and with the world around them? What are the strengths and challenges of this new posture? How would leadership in this new "place" look? These are ques-tions that we consider as we move to the second of this model's four postures.

Notes

1. Jane Addams, "The Objective Value of a Social Settlement," in *Phi-lanthropy and Social Progress* (New York: Thomas Y. Crowell and Co., 1893), 28–30, as quoted in Jean Bethke Elshtain, *Jane Addams and the Dream of American Democracy* (New York: Basic Books, 2002), 98.

2. Ibid., xv.

3. For general information on the development of African American churches, their theology and way of life, see C. Eric Lincoln and Lawrence H. Mamiya, The *Black Church in the African American Experience* (Durham: Duke University Press, 1990), and James H. Evans, Jr., *We Have Been Believers: An African-American Systematic Theology* (Minneapolis: Fortress Press, 1992).

4. For a concise statement on this point, see Andrew M. Greeley, *Why Can't They Be Like Us? America's White Ethnic Groups* (New York: E.P. Dutton & Co., 1971), esp. the first three chapters.

5. A sophisticated version of organizational lifecycle theory is pre-sented in Ichak Adizes, *Corporate Lifecycles: How and Why Corpo-rations Grow and Die and What to Do About It* (Englewood Cliffs: Prentice-Hall, 1988).

6. An explanation of the nature, role and importance of a congre-gation's "assumptions" in its own culture is found in my book, *How to Get Along with Your Pastor: Creating Partnership for Doing Ministry* (Cleveland: The Pilgrim Press, 2006), ch. 1.

7. To read about these various "levels of culture" and why incon-sistencies occur in organizations, see Edgar Schein, *The Corporate*

Culture Survival Guide (San Francisco: Jossey-Bass, 1999), ch. 1; reading the case studies on 69–86 is a helpful way to see Schein's culture analysis at work.

8. Floyd Massey, Jr., and Samuel Berry McKinney, *Church Administration in the Black Perspective* (Valley Forge: Judson Press, 1976), 23–24.

9. See, for instance, E. Digby Baltzell, *The Protestant Establishment: Aristocracy and Caste in America* (New York: Random House, 1964).

CHAPTER 4

Middle of Anywhere

The Most Common Place to Get Stuck

INNER-DIRECTED CONVENTIONALITY

Anywhere as Everywhere

My hometown, I suppose, is like many other American towns. Founded in the mid-nineteenth century, it became the county seat and constructed a stone courthouse building in 1889—one of those dark grey structures that seems inspired by medieval castles or cathedrals. It sits on the square in the center of downtown, as do so many thousands of other courthouses in thousands of other nineteenth-century towns established across the United States. Later, city hall was built across from the courthouse square's southeastern corner, and behind it the original firehouse. The local newspaper's offices have been located just west of city hall for as long as I can remember. An auto dealership sits across the street to the northeast, with another lot for cars to its north. The old theater north of the courthouse is now closed, but it is surrounded by small businesses on either side, businesses that have come and gone over the decades. Main Street borders the courthouse square on the west, with a row of buildings, wall to wall, originally constructed in the 1870s and 1880s. A jeweler, a restaurant, the 88-cent store, a gift store, and two pharmacies occupied that block when I was growing up.

Back in those days, Main Street was two-way, so the high school dropouts and other "hoods" drove their enviable, raked-up '57 Chevys and '56 Fords up and down Main from late afternoon into the evening. I worked in the Rexall pharmacy in high school. Most of its customers were employed at the mills or farmed outside of town. Men in suits were much less common: they either had business in the courthouse or were passing through town.

Around the perimeter of the courthouse square there was only one saloon, but the presence of many others throughout the rest of town more than made up for it. Taverns and bars hugged the property lines of the mills on both ends of town, and there seemed to be plenty of these liquor-dispensing establishments in between, too. I never knew if any of my school mates had parents who frequented these bars, but that ignorance probably reflected the social proprieties of the times. I never thought much about them, though. There was another institution in town that seemed to garner more respect—at least publicly.

In the years that I was growing up, my hometown grew in population from about 5,000 to 7,000 persons. Every week, the local paper ran a Church Directory section, a list that included anywhere between 40 and 50 places of worship. Admittedly, some of them were located out of town, on winding roads and with addresses from even smaller hamlets. Still, as I discovered in later years, this number of churches is quite large for the size of the town! How was it that so many churches existed alongside so many taverns in this logging and farming county?

The Stuff of "Anywhere"

Part of the answer to this question is the subject of this chapter. Among these many congregations, a few probably began life in the inner-directed marginality posture. The Assembly of God congregation I mentioned in the previous chapter is one of those. It is not surprising in a working-class community to find congregations here and there striving to help people on the edge survive. Yet what strikes me about these churches is their self-absorbed satisfaction. Many of the churches in my hometown had existed for decades; they worshipped and maintained other typical church activities in facilities of some age; their sense of place and their energy levels had reached a plateau. Their focus of identity was not particularly different than those of inner-directed marginality. What distinguished them from newer, struggling congregations was their conventionality.

In this chapter, we learn more about such inner-directed conventionality. As one quadrant on the contextual posture grid, inner-directed conventionality holds one element in common with one of the other quadrants and another element in common with a third quadrant. Recognizing both the one basic similarity and the one basic difference helps us to appreciate how the grid itself identifies particular features of church life that otherwise might be missed. Whereas inner-directed *marginal* churches wrestle with their unchosen, difficult place in the world, inner-directed *conventional* churches are much more at ease with their place. Inner-directed conventional churches feel relatively satisfied with themselves and the way that things are. They are self-absorbed. In this way, inner-directed conventional churches are fairly "standard brand"; they could be in the middle of anywhere. This is where we find them on the contextual posture grid.

My hometown offers the kind of context that would encourage this posture to thrive. You probably know others. Perhaps you live in one. In many ways, my hometown is typical of many other established American communities. Following the anguish and horror of World War II, the nation wanted to get back to the business of living again. Soldiers returned home and started raising families: the Baby Boom began. Many towns and suburbs grew, others were founded, people moved to them, and churches were established. Most middle-class, white suburban Protestant congregations came into being in communities where they eventually fit in fine. Working hard, enjoying life and fitting in were all values to pursue. Many, if not most, Americans were not raising questions of deeper meaning. For goodness' sake, the Depression was over, the war was over! There was no need to rock the boat.[1]

American life in the early post-World War II period illustrates qualities of identity and position that characterize churches in inner-directed conventionality. These churches share with the churches described in the previous chapter an inward-focused identity. The primary interest in both cases is in the select community that such churches seek to maintain and sustain. In this chapter, however, we distinguish a quadrant in which the congregation already has established a way to fit in with its world. It is not struggling for survival or basic social place but to maintain its boundaries. This is why this quadrant is termed "inner-directed conventionality."

Fitting In

Such congregations do not make waves. What is known of them publicly is considered respectable enough, even if their theology and religious practice happen to possess some purported challenge to the status quo. Their actual participation in matters of the public arena is as second- or third-tier performers, politely and sometimes tepidly following someone else's lead. It is thus fitting, and not necessarily judgmental, to refer to them as "self-absorbed."

Congregations who live in the inner-directed conventional posture could be anywhere in society, because their stance toward the world can be interpreted as indifferent. Not only this, their location "anywhere" is in the middle: they are not forced to exist socially and economically on some precarious edge. They can afford to be self-absorbed because they participate sufficiently in their environment's social and economic stability— whatever that is like in their context. As noted in chapter 2, I estimate that about half or more of all American Christian congregations today are living out of this posture—proportionately far more than any of the other three quadrants or postures.

Inner-directed conventionality provides persons in these churches with weekly worship that, to long-time members, is familiar and comforting. Networks of relationships nurture members and their families, and most of the congregation's activities serve this purpose. It is not unusual for inner-directed conventional churches to offer a warm welcome to visitors. Those who stay and eventually join, however, discover that they usually do not move into the center of the congregation's life. This limited capacity for newcomers to be admitted into social and cultural space reflects a key quality of the church that is both inner-

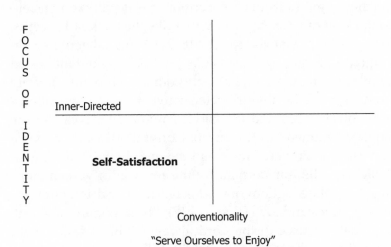

STANCE WITH WORLD

F
O
C
U
S

O
F   Inner-Directed

I
D
E
N   **Self-Satisfaction**
T
I
T
Y

Conventionality

"Serve Ourselves to Enjoy"
CHURCH IN THE MIDDLE OF ANYWHERE

directed and conventional. Its self-absorption—a relative complacence with the way that things are—fosters little new energy, certainly not the kind that reaches beyond established relationships to enlarge the circle of the church's witness.

Inner-directed conventionality seems to describe a large share of American congregations today. For their members, these churches have become comfortable places to gather weekly, for special events, to affirm their belief in a God of care and security, to celebrate community and the passages of life. Even for churches with an evangelical heritage, the subtleties that come with settling into routines and familiar behaviors, without notice, can take the edge off the church's fervor. Regardless of its theological stripe, a church ostrich in inner-directed conventionality is one happy camper. It sees no need for a lemonade stand, since it does not pay much attention to the lemons around it.

Encouraging the Comfortable

Just as churches in inner-directed marginality resonate with certain biblical texts and theological themes, so also do churches in inner-directed conventionality. Because they are settled in their niche in society, these congregations focus upon issues of life within their community of faith. Sermons easily will exhort listeners to the kind of practical advice that fills the book of Proverbs. Watching out for what you say (12:18, 22), being diligent in what you do (10:4), forgiving others (17:9), not being more interested in wealth than reputation (22:1), and other such points of daily wisdom reinforce the inner-directed conventional congregation's attitude toward itself and its world. Pauline directives, not the theological arguments of Romans or Corinthians, are as quotable and portable as Proverbs for strengthening the faith and life of the believers. "Be transformed by the renewal of your minds" (Rom. 12:2); "the kingdom of God is not food or drink but righteousness, peace and joy" (Rom. 14:17); "Be strong in the Lord" (Eph. 6:10a); "Rejoice in the Lord always" (Phil. 4:4a);" "Fight the good fight of the faith" (1 Tim. 6:12a). These and similar texts serve as short-hand reinforcement of a faith that is already figured out and primarily calls only for obedience.

The life of an inner-directed conventional church offers stability, status, and affirmation, especially to its long-time members. They are more interested in what they think of themselves than of what their community thinks of them. Indeed, as the years go by, inner-directed conventional churches might hold a perception of their place in the community that is very different than reality. Deep down, the congregation believes that "we have what we want" and "we are content to be who we are." Beyond commenting to visitors that "we are warm and friendly," members of these churches say little out loud about what is important to the congregation. Their budget typically includes mission projects locally and beyond, but a newcomer to the church might feel that these are token gestures. In inner-directed conventionality, a church's energy and concentration clearly is on itself (however it defines itself) rather than upon the needs of persons and groups in difficult circumstances. Their efforts to interact with people in need are often brief and ill-considered. We can speculate that the culture of inner-directed conventionality makes it awkward and nervous for a church that is content with itself to wrestle deeply with segments of its world for which contentment is elusive.

Entry Points

Congregations arrive in the posture of inner-directed conventionality from more than one entry point, but it is generally through one of three ways: from the church's beginning, and from one of two of the other quadrants. These distinctions are instructive to note.

Some congregations in inner-directed conventionality seem to have started out that way. Consider, for instance, suburban churches that were established in the years following World War II. Because their communities were growing steadily, and because the nature of suburban life tends to support conventional sociability, most of these churches never were marginal at their beginnings. They emerged as mirrors of their social and cultural contexts and thus started out in the inner-directed conventional quadrant. It also appears that many, if not most, of them have remained there.

Other congregations have arrived at inner-directed conventionality through its struggling sibling quadrant inner-directed marginality. A look at some of the churches in inner-directed conventionality provides enough evidence to argue that they began on an edge, not in the middle. American history provides us with ample such evidence. In the nineteenth and early twentieth centuries, many white ethnic waves of immigration led to the establishment of new local churches (and sometimes of denominations) within these ethnic groups. Especially in the North, many Scandinavian and German settlers moved to America for opportunity, only to discover the challenges of language, customs, and prejudice. Their churches were founded in part as refuges from the storms created by social and economic marginalization and as a continuation of whatever religious group the immigrants left. In church, the native tongue was retained, old relationships of kin and friendship stabilized and supported the members, and traditional customs celebrated the cherished homeland.

As the generations went by, however, the families who constituted many of these congregations gradually moved closer into the social mainstream. Their children and grandchildren learned to speak English flawlessly; some in the second and third generations did not have to work in the factories but started businesses of their own; the families began to purchase homes and live in nicer neighborhoods; a few of their children managed to attend college. In some important respects, life got easier. This shift from the edges into the wider middle of society did (and does) not occur quickly, easily, or automatically. Yet many white ethnic groups in America have made that transition to one degree or another. They eventually survive the challenging early years of attracting a committed membership and garnering adequate resources for ongoing activity. As their place in society becomes more stable, so do their churches. In the terms of this book, such congregations have moved from marginality to conventionality. What we have described here is a move that retains the inner-directed identity.

By contrast, still other congregations could have moved into inner-directed conventionality for a return stint. In these cases, the churches in question earlier in their lives would have been located in the empathetic conventional quadrant (which we will discuss in the following chapter). Over a period of some years, churches like this can lose their empathetic spirit. They could move away from their ability and genuine desire to relate their ministry to issues and needs that exist beyond their immediate church community. Even though a change like this is not calculated or even conscious, it can and does occur. The significance of this shift "back" to an inner-directed ethos should become more apparent in the next chapter.

Conventional Leading

Congregations living out of inner-directed conventionality do not seek leadership. This statement might sound like a harsh assessment, yet it is consistent with what we find. If "leading" is presumed merely to consist of maintaining activities and services to the satisfaction of long-time members, we could conclude that churches in inner-directed marginality possess some leadership. Yet I agree with those who say that leadership is something different,[2] and this difference is why churches in this posture see, or welcome, so little leadership.

Leadership has more to do with helping a community or organization pursue a worthwhile vision, with integrity.[3] Churches in inner-directed conventionality can be caring communities of faith, with high ethical standards and filled with nurturing activities. They can be all this but not even know that they confuse initiative, activity, and achievement with leading. Their ethos draws them back in on themselves and upon their proclivity for upholding what they consider standard practice. Hence, their sense of what they need is limited and in the long run will not serve them.

Instead, churches in inner-directed conventionality face the challenge to embrace a larger sense of the Gospel and from there to move into empathy. As we saw in chapter 2, two of the postures in this grid are inner-directed and two are empathetic. The easier move for inner-directed conventional churches is to the empathetic posture of conventionality. This is because the energy and commitment required to move from an inner-directed stance to an empathetic stance is less than the energy and commitment required to move from conventionality to marginality.

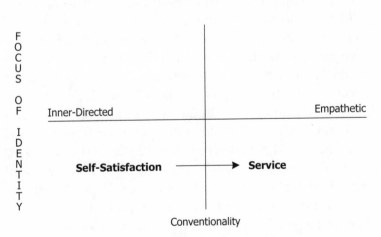

The easier move for inner-directed conventionality;
hence, the challenge for leading

Making the Case for a Move

Why should a church in inner-directed conventionality venture out of its familiar and comfortable niche? I believe that there are both pragmatic (realistic and practical) and normative (theological and idealistic) reasons that would compel it to move. For one thing, churches in inner-directed conventionality are not simply trying to survive. They represent a church population that, generally speaking, does not live hand-to-mouth. They have access to more than the minimum. Although they certainly are not immune to crises and tragedies in life, they are not in dire straits. Their congregational resources are more than sufficient. They have enough and then some of a physical plant, income, and human talents and skills. As an organization, the inner-directed conventional church does not take; it has enough to give.

These reasons alone are not compelling, however. What catapults a community of faith into something new and taxing tends to be a fresh understanding of its calling. That calling finds its legitimacy in biblical and theological claims, claims that the inner-directed conventional church somehow hears and receives as it previously had not. No one particular biblical text or story will give rise to such a new hearing; no particular religious slogan can take credit for turning the inner-directed conventional church toward empathy. The congregation might hear Matthew 25:40—"just as you did it to one of the least of these who are members of my family, you did it to me"—and conclude that they have not answered God's call fully. They might become aware of the Hebrew Bible's witness to the LORD's special concern for the welfare of three categories of people—widows, orphans, and "strangers" (those living in Israel but of another nationality) (see Exodus 22:21–23; Psalm 146:9; Jeremiah 7:5–6; Ezekiel 22:7)— and be stirred. References abound in the Scriptures to the theme of God's intention that the chosen people become a light to others, a blessing for all of God's creatures. Taking this theme to heart would spur a church to become empathetic.

What happens to a congregation that undergoes this, or any, move from one posture to another is at least a shift in interpretive frameworks. Whether they consciously realize it or not, the church members are changing their way of understanding life with God. They hear in a new and different way both the Bible as normative ("the way that things should be") and the world around them as descriptive ("the way that things actually are"). Once such a process of reframing begins to happen, it is unlikely that the church can stand still. On paper, then, there is great potential here. Since a majority of today's churches exist in inner-directed conventionality, this shift would release significant energy for ministry beyond one's walls.

Stimulus

So what would stimulate a church in inner-directed conventionality to begin such a journey? How might a satisfied ostrich, in the middle of somewhere, decide to do something about lemons? There is no simple formula for achieving such a move of postures, but several particular factors can be involved, regardless of the exact process. For one, some respected member could identify a sense of the congregation's stagnation, that it has flattened out, that its energy has become too predictable. For another, changes in the church's immediate neighborhood and community could enter the church's conversation. Perhaps older residents are moving out and younger ones moving in; perhaps the housing market is changing dramatically; perhaps a different ethnic group is more visible on the streets and in the stores. Recognizing any contextual changes then could lead, if the church is willing to be honest, to self-examination about its life and future: who are we, and what is our mission? How effective such a conversation is depends mainly on the degree of trust and respect among the church's members. If their *esprit de corps* has eroded, discussions that identify or question the church's inner-directedness or its conventionality can quickly turn confrontational and conflictual.

I am quite sure that motivating a congregation to change postures will not happen through preaching alone. Pastors often assume that what they say in the pulpit carries such import and esteem that words themselves move the congregation to act. For pastors, I have addressed this and other issues in another book.[4] In my experience as a pastor and a seminary professor, I have heard plenty of stories of preachers who have shot themselves in the foot from the pulpit. More pastors need to take Eric Law's advice from his interpretation of Acts 2. Law points out that the Pentecost coming of the Holy Spirit was a wonder both of speaking and of hearing. Pastors who want to help their congregations would do well to do a lot of listening to the church members during the week. Pastoral calling, board and committee meetings, Bible studies, fellowship dinners, and other church events and activities provide valuable opportunities to listen—if the pastor is astute enough to do so. That hearing can then guide the pastor's preparation to preach.[5] This advice is especially helpful for inner-directed conventional churches, since they do not expect their pastors to do anything out of the ordinary.

The Danger of Fitting In

One young pastor whom I met through a training project was struggling with his ministry in a new congregation. He had been called there only a little more than a year earlier, from a different region of the country. Pastor and congregation seemed to like each other; their theologies appeared generally compatible; and Pastor Don's lifestyle fit in well with their small-town farming community. But Pastor Don felt as though he was running into apathy and passive resistance. The story that he learned of the congregation's history, and the opportunities that he saw for them,[6] illustrate a typical pattern of movement across the contextual posture grid. This pattern links together the three church postures that are discussed in the previous chapter, the present chapter and the upcoming chapter.

Lord Jesus Church was founded some years after the immigration of its founders from Russia to the American Great Plains. Descendants of German Pietists, these immigrants' grandparents had been driven out of Germany because their religious beliefs and practices did not fit in with the state church of their day. Then the humble group was forced out of Russia as well.

Eventually they sailed for America, and in due course one contingent of their group ended up in the wide open spaces of the far Midwest.

Early life in their new home was not much different than their life as peasant farmers had been in Germany and Russia. Large landowners hired these Pietist men to work their vast fields and provided housing for their families. It did not take long for the children of owner and serf to mingle during playtime. On one such occasion, a terrible accident occurred. All the children were playing next to one of the long irrigation ditches for the fields when the landowner's young daughter fell in. The peasant children tried to rescue her, but she drowned. Quickly, the other children ran to their mothers and reported the awful tragedy. Word spread quickly. When the landowner heard the news and retrieved his daughter's body, he was so grief-stricken that he ordered the family of the children with whom his daughter had been playing off of his land immediately.

Now reeling with back-to-back shocks, they headed down the road toward another peasant family's house. By the time they had arrived there, however, their father decided to go back and ask the landowner for some time to pack up their belongings. His wife tried to talk him out of this idea, fearing for his life. He went anyway. As he was walking up the dirt road toward the landowner's house, the grieving father inside saw him approaching. Picking up a rifle, he went out in front of his house and took aim at the peasant man coming to negotiate with him. Without warning, he fired a shot, and the dedicated farm worker fell to the dust with a fatal bullet wound.

According to the oral tradition of Lord Jesus Church, this murder of one of their ancestors was never prosecuted or investigated. Yet somehow their close-knit band managed to remain in the general area and survive. They founded their church, they raised their children. As years went by, their descendants were settling into the community that was growing in the region's rolling hills. Before World War II began, they had constructed a brick church structure with a semicircular sanctuary and balcony. It was their pride and joy. Some of the members now owned their own farms; a few members had studied at college; one member had been elected to a state office. Their town, the county seat, was growing; small subdivisions began appearing on the edges of the annexation boundaries.

This growth in population was fueled primarily by families whose men and women were hired at the local poultry packing plant. These families had been born in another country and spoke a language other than English. Some of them were renting dingy houses near Lord Jesus Church. During the week, one could hear unfamiliar music and smell unfamiliar cooking aromas coming from those houses. Among the church's membership, no conversation about their new neighbors had taken place. Perhaps it was just a coincidence that one of the most respected members of the congregation had mentioned here and there the idea of constructing a new church out on the edge of town.

No wonder Pastor Don was struggling. As a newcomer, he could see opportunities that the congregation saw but did not interpret the same way. In order to lead this congregation, Pastor Don had to find ways to gain its respect and earn its trust. If Lord Jesus Church ever was going to gain empathy, it would not be because its pastor pestered or shamed them into it.[7] The Pentecost image of hearing could help Pastor Don discover more about this self-absorbed congregation. Until it had claimed its own story and named its own dreams, the church would have no energy for a move of postures.

Facing Opportunity—and Call

The story of Lord Jesus Church touches on three of the grid's contextual postures and prepares us for chapter 5. To outsiders like us, it might seem quite ironic that a congregation with a painful history of injustice and social marginality seemingly could turn a deaf ear to its town's new marginal people. We are using the contextual posture grid to help us understand these kinds of realities, but also to help our churches learn how to move out of them. The story of their ancestor's murder had lost its edge. Indeed, one of Lord Jesus Church's matrons told me that this story never had been discussed publicly: it had been passed down privately from generation to generation, as though it were something of which to be ashamed.

Yet, here is a success story that could go sour. Lord Jesus Church gradually had moved out of inner-directed marginality into inner-directed conventionality, a move to stability that strengthens the congregation's potential for ministry. At the same time, it was its inner-directed focus that made it difficult for the congregation to use its own history to identify with the strange-speaking, strange-smelling folks moving into town to work the jobs that none of their families wanted. Ostrich-style energy needs more than a nudge to wake up and direct itself to the business of making lemonade.

When new things appear in their immediate world, inner-directed conventional churches stay the course. The ethos of their contented posture works against their capacity for hearing the gospel speak to them in their new situation. In a nutshell, this is the danger for inner-directed conventional churches. Though they might do so, the world around them does not stand still.

Let us next explore the promise of what happens when churches who fit into their world nonetheless find a way to reach out.

Notes

1. This phenomenon did not develop without a contemporary critique. Theologian Langdon Gilkey was concerned that congregations early in the 1960s were "in danger of capitulating completely to the status quo." He observed increasing numbers of churches following middle-class movement to suburbs, turning into "Sunday School fellowships," disconnected from urban life, where suburbanites worked and observed evidences of society's cutting edges. See Langdon Gilkey, *How the Church Can Minister to the World Without Losing Itself* (New York: Harper & Row, 1964), 46. Gilkey's comments parallel those of Gibson Winter's, whom he cites and whose critique of post-World War II American Protestantism is mentioned above in chapter 2.

2. For a concise and lucid distinguishing of leadership from other forms of activity, see Lovett H. Weems, Jr., *Church Leadership: Vision, Team, Culture and Integrity* (Nashville: Abingdon Press, 1993), 34–35.

3. Ibid., ch. 2, esp. 54–55, for a helpful orientation to the notion of vision as applied to congregations.

4. See my *How to Get Along with Your Church: Creating Cultural Capital for Doing Ministry* (Cleveland: The Pilgrim Press, 2001), esp. chs. 2, 4, and 5 (becoming accepted, dealing with bad news, and leadership).

5. Eric H. F. Law, *The Wolf Shall Dwell with the Lamb: A Spirituality for Leadership in a Multicultural Community* (St. Louis: Chalice Press, 1993), 46–47.

6. I have written of this story elsewhere, in *Treasures in Clay Jars: New Ways to Understand Your Church* (Cleveland: The Pilgrim Press, 2003), 17–20, in terms of sociological categories.

7. For an extended discussion of how a pastor can help a church come to terms with dynamics that it is reluctant to address, see my book, *How to Get Along with Your Pastor: Creating Cultural Capital for Doing Ministry* (Cleveland: The Pilgrim Press, 2001), ch. 4, "Bad News."

CHAPTER 5

Middle of Somewhere

The More Common Move Beyond Ourselves

EMPATHETIC CONVENTIONALITY

When Piety Hits the Streets

You have heard the charge—and you have squirmed in discomfort. A pastor writes an article claiming that churches have become plump, more concerned about their appearance, their church buildings, and their organs than for their cities' "underground classes."[1] A group of highly respected professors speaks in clear terms about wealth in the church and reminds us that one of the main missions for churches is to assist those in poverty and who are oppressed.[2] Yes, chimes in another voice, alleviating poverty is one of the church's three historic purposes, and American churches are at risk of totally forsaking the lowest classes of society.[3] A preacher in Boston warns that religion is being challenged by the growing numbers of destitute persons in our cities.[4]

Some church members and churches have responded to such challenges—perhaps including you and yours. They have organized to help find employment for adults and places to live for abandoned children and teenagers. They have set up deliveries of food, clothing, and cash to impoverished families. In one city alone, this ecumenical effort involved dozens of congregations and more than 5,000 volunteers working with other agencies.[5] Others have visited prisons, while still others have secured buildings to use for sleeping, job training, education, and worship. Their clientele includes new immigrants to the land of the free.[6]

Those who participate in these charitable activities are inspired by preaching that sees the Kingdom of God on its way, as personal faith flows out into action for social progress—especially among "the least of these."[7]

These initiatives to engage in poverty's struggles for survival as an expression of faith certainly do sound strikingly contemporary. Those of us who are old enough to remember the 1960s were exposed to prophetic preaching. We were reminded of the biblical witness to God's concern for "the stranger, the widow, and the orphan," three categories of persons in antiquity who were especially vulnerable (and of course still are). Some of our churches in those days took youth mission "plunges" into the city, showing sheltered suburban and small-town teens something of the complexity of the urban scene. These trips often were led by a seminary student with a zeal for expanding the congregation's horizons about what Christian ministry could be.

This zeal, though, was too frequently limited and short-lived. To many of us in the sixties, it seemed that the biblical call to care for those in need had been thrust in the faces of American churches for the first time.

These calls for Christian social involvement and the resulting extensively organized efforts, however, did not occur during our lifetime. Unexpected as it might seem, this ministry to the "down and out" in American cities actually took place more than 150 years ago, in the early part of the 1800s! The pastors, preachers, evangelists, professors, and lay people to whom we have alluded spoke, wrote, and established these forms of ministry during the generation before the Civil War. A revival had spread across the United States, throughout virtually every Protestant denomination of the time. It was particularly well-received in America's growing, newly industrialized cities, with well-educated pastors and church members of substantial resources. This revival was not just about converting the individual soul. It was also about a new age being ushered in, as the well-being of all people improved. Personal piety went hand in hand, these impassioned leaders argued, with action to alleviate suffering and bring dignity to everyone.

Does this little history lesson surprise you? It is easy for us to look at things through the lenses of our own limited experience, perspective, and place in history. If we are serious about our faith, there will be times in life when we are drawn up short and have to face a new challenge from God. Otherwise, we could be doomed to triviality, as the world and its cries for salvation go unnoticed.

The "Feeling-with" Church

This chapter deals with what it takes for congregations to learn to hear and respond to the world's cries for help. This book's contextual posture grid for understanding the ethos of congregations offers one particular way to identify how congregations see themselves, how they listen, and how they act out their faith. In the previous two chapters, we considered general characteristics of churches that are inner-directed. Whether they fit into their community and context or not, inner-directed churches position their identity primarily toward themselves. Their behavior is driven by concern to meet their own perceived needs and interests.

By contrast, this chapter and the following one describe churches on the other end of the "stance toward identity" continuum—the end that I have termed "empathetic." Empathy literally means "to feel with." Congregations with empathy express the capacity to care about those beyond themselves, because their understanding of identity and purpose points beyond themselves. Those American churches in the 1840s and 1850s that were touched by revival discovered that their rekindled faith generated considerable empathy. It takes empathy for ostriches to pay attention to the lemons around them and then decide to do something about it.

In this chapter, we see how the empathetic quality interacts with the "conventional" side of the "stance toward world" continuum. This interaction creates a congregation that is at home in its environment yet deliberately reaches beyond itself in the

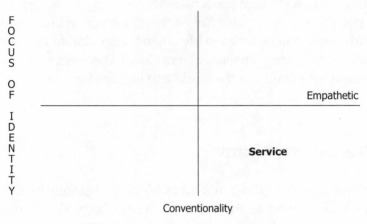

"Serve Others with Our Abundance"
CHURCH IN THE MIDDLE OF SOMEWHERE

name of Christ. Empathetic conventional churches give of their resources to provide services that meet the immediate needs of people in crisis. For this reason, this posture is called "the middle of somewhere," since these congregations engage the world from their position of wellbeing and security. Whereas its inner-directed cousin is characterized by self-absorption, the empathetic conventional church is rightly distinguished by service.

A typical list of the kinds of service ministries in which an empathetic conventional church would be involved will sound familiar. It is not that churches in this posture are the only ones to do this work; it is rather that their motivation, their energy, and often their results in so doing are striking. Think Meals on Wheels deliveries; serving at soup kitchens; donating to and volunteering at clothes closets and food pantries; after-school mentoring; youth recreation; mission trips to other parts of the country and to other nations; sponsoring recovery groups; substantial budget items for local, national, and international mission support; and lobbying city councilpersons or state legislators on matters of public safety, child care, and the like. If someone can imagine it, the empathetic conventional church is probably doing it. Even its worship and educational ministries will be infused with empathy. Minutes for mission will be a regular feature of Sunday worship; Sunday School classes will study variations on the theme of loving your neighbor as yourself.

Because empathetic conventional churches are so active and fairly energetic, their expectations for their church members are often perceived as stronger than certain other churches. Certainly it is not difficult to imagine that churches in the inner-directed conventional posture (the previous chapter) communicate a more relaxed view of involvement. As long as members fit in to customary behavior patterns and activities, they will be readily accepted. That kind of congregation, as we have seen in the previous chapter, does not look for new things. On the empathetic side of the conventional coin, however, membership seems imbued with an understanding of participation that tends to be more defined and active. Rather than obliging them to serve, its spirit of empathy inspires people to do so. Members, and even regular non-members, tend to be more willing to get involved.

Biblical and Cultural Characteristics

Certain biblical texts and theological themes undergird and symbolize the spirit of empathetic conventional churches. They hear Jesus' words at the end of Matthew 25 as a call to action for today: "for I was hungry ... I was thirsty ... I was a stranger ... I was naked ... I was sick ... I was in prison ... and you ..." (35–37). They are not intimidated when they hear such Old Testament utterances as "if you do not oppress the alien, the orphan, and the widow . . . then I will dwell with you in this place" (Jeremiah 7:6–7). Many of these texts are part of the stream of biblical tradition out of which the four Gospels portray Jesus' teaching about mercy and compassion. In this sense, empathetic conventional churches tend to "hear" more of the Bible. They weave together—sometimes quite imaginatively—care for vulnerable members of society, fair dealings in the public arena, and a life of genuine worship and holy living (e.g., Ezekiel 22:6–12). Their empathetic ethos creates an ability to pay attention to texts and themes that call faithful communities beyond themselves, to outward action.

Because these congregations have tapped into a heart for the well-being of others, their energy tends to be contagious. Everything they do exudes an air of welcome and invitation—Sunday worship, educational programs, study groups, and so on. Thus, these congregations are likely to attract visitors, some of whom will get involved and eventually become members. The empathy appeals to church seekers who respond to warmth linked with a cause. These are congregations whose activities easily make connections to mission.

The cultural ethos of empathetic conventional churches reflects some common characteristics but also some common historical patterns. It is not unusual to hear in their stories tales of earlier periods of decline and reckoning. These congregations not infrequently have endured a period of uncertainty. Often this occurs as a consequence of significant changes in the church's neighborhood or town. Their decision to reach out into the community thus becomes deliberate, sowing the seeds for a new era of congregational openness and flexibility. Members try new projects and discover that they are effective and satisfying. This success creates it own momentum and becomes contagious. Members are happy to invite and welcome others, because they feel little threat to their church's way of life. When the congregation affirms its identity with sayings like "God calls us to spread Christ's love beyond our doors," they mean it. Deep down, beyond the obvious activities and slogans, these congregations hold even deeper beliefs, the ones that drive them. Unspoken but strongly defining beliefs such as "we have something to offer," "people who are different from us are still important," "new members have room to get involved and try out new things" provide the foundation for everything that such a congregation does. At its best, the empathetic conventional church has few "land mines" that would surprise a new pastor or church member.

"Old First Church"

With such characteristics as these, what does an empathetic conventional church look like? Think about some twentieth-century versions of the congregations mentioned at the beginning of this chapter. In the middle of the previous century, many American towns and cities had Protestant churches in or near the middle of town, in large, impressive stone or brick structures. Such congregations had been part of their communities for a few generations and more. The neighborhoods around these churches were thriving. These churches had the resources and reputation to attract pastors with crowd appeal. Their memberships included school principals, city council members, successful business owners, and the like. These churches influenced the life of their communities, through direct participation in civic events and indirect participation, too—as their members became active in aid societies, PTA, and so on. Then, the Baby Boom (1946-1964) began to fill up Sunday School rooms so quickly that many congregations added separate educational facilities. At that point, it looked as though these congregations truly had it made.

If we fast-forward a generation, we find Old First Church on the other side of the tumultuous civil rights era of American history. Lunchroom counter protests in Atlanta, school integration, Dr. King's "I Have a Dream" speech on the Washington Mall, college sit-ins protesting the Vietnam War, the sexual revolution, the first walk on the moon, the Watergate scandal—such events from that era have marked changes in American society that still reverberate in every town and city today. The outlook for many Old First Churches now is less rosy than it used to be. Their communities often changed ethnic and economic demographics; new members joined less frequently, longtime members aged, youth grew up and moved away. What has happened to their spirit of empathy? Have they been able to maintain it, in spite of contextual factors that are not as favorable?

Often they did not. As its resources steadily waned, Old First Church was just as likely to have slipped back into a focus upon itself (see the end of chapter 4). Yet some of these longtime stalwarts were able to come to grips with their new situation. They worked through their fears and listened to the Bible afresh. They looked beyond the details of disagreements and conflicts to underlying issues. They recommitted themselves to ministry in their community. They took a few risks and did not shrink from failure. In other words, they pulled their heads out of the sand and chose to build a lemonade stand. Although Old First Church often has not returned to the same high levels of attendance, membership, general resources, and community status it once enjoyed, it still has something to give—to its members, its guests, and its community.

Leading and the Grid

A number of the points described here imply some specific things about the role of leadership. As we will see in the final chapter, leadership is more than staying busy or keeping things going. It is crucial to maintain this distinction, since assumptions about leading will affect a congregation's long-term vitality. Churches located in any one of the four contextual postures of this grid can be busy with all kinds of activities. However, to find leadership, we have to look beyond sheer bustle. Not only this, but leadership actually looks different from posture to posture. This key dynamic is not understood much at all in American society: we continue to be enamored instead with the image of the "great person" whose determination and personal style of initiative seem to make things happen on their own, no matter what.[8] A church's deliberate movement from one contextual posture to another indeed does require leading, but leading is not based on imitation or borrowing—and certainly not simply on raw will.

Consider this comparison: the vision that leadership in an inner-directed marginal church pursues is one of providing authentic dignity and accomplishment to a faith community living in circumstances that are challenging. To lead this kind of church takes risk and courage. By contrast, shifting out of this posture into inner-directed conventionality does not take leadership (articulating and pursuing vision) as much as it does management (organizing and stabilizing resources).[9] From there, crossing into the empathetic side of conventionality takes leadership, since an inner-directed church's ethos does not change easily. Even an appeal to specific biblical texts or a theology that supports empathetic ministries will not stimulate this shift by itself (much to the surprise and discouragement of many a preacher!).

Instead, strategies must fit the dynamics of each distinct posture. Because any shift entails a different combination of the "world" and "identity" stances, leadership necessarily faces different tests (we will discuss this point even further in the final two chapters).

For many church members, observing the factors that create and maintain an empathetic conventional congregation would satisfy their expectation of leadership. The pastor and influential church members need to be consistent in word and deed about their commitment to a gospel that serves others. This expansive aim would involve a few basic and interrelated objectives. For one, it would be essential to continue to articulate and interpret the congregation's vision as a uniting element. Congregations do not stand still, even when they are positioned squarely in the middle of one or another of the postures. Inertia pulls against the energy of empathy unless it is periodically renewed.

This ferment, generated as it is from a renewal of empathy, then also helps the congregation to assess its ministries, redefining and expanding as it sees fit. Assessment, evaluation, and adjustments grow out of some form of extended congregational conversations that are encouraged and channeled. Because it loves out of empathy, congregations in this posture are challenged to continue to pay attention to any changes in their world. If they get stuck in ruts, current activities and programs become ends in themselves. By asking itself again and again about its motivation for meeting needs outside its doors, the empathetic conventional church can avoid drifting toward the "inner-directed" boundary line of identity.

Such a rhythm of renewal will help the congregation experience its inner life and its outward mission as *yin* and *yang*—as ostensible opposites that in fact are indivisible. To many members of these churches, empathetic conventionality feels like "arriving." It seems as though their church is about as good as it gets. Officers, staff, and active members typically share a sense of ongoing accomplishment that usually is fairly assessed. Empathetic conventional churches often achieve notable results in their various forms of ministry.

There is danger, of course, that the two foci of fellowship and mission will drift apart, which usually means that the internal interest of "being comfortable with ourselves" ends up dominating. The congregation becomes ever-so-subtly tempted to hide like an ostrich behind a lemonade stand or two that have become quite comfortable. When this occurs the congregation will have shifted postures. For many of them, moving into the inner-directed quadrant of conventionality means a move "back" to where they used to be. This shift from the "middle of somewhere" to the "middle of anywhere" represents a loss of ministry and vitality. Thus, leadership in the empathetic conventional posture calls for a certain kind of diligence just to maintain strength of focus.

Having said all this here, however, our journey is not complete. Congregational empathy can take another form as well. What kind of energy would it take for even this outgoing, resourceful congregation to make the move out of conventionality and into marginality?

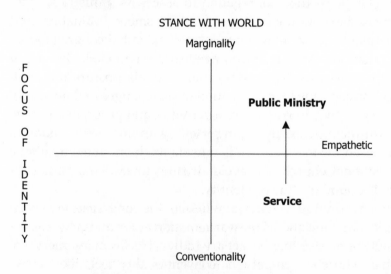

The harder move from empathetic conventionality
to empathetic marginality

Empathetic marginality is rare, because it requires more from the congregation than any of the other three postures do. Many congregations that make it to empathetic conventionality will do well to stay there. In the terms of this book, they will have found a way to engage some part of the world with gospel ministry. What they will *not* have found is a way to move out of their own comfort zone and engage the world with a kind of holy energy that derives only by living from an edge.

Notes

1. Timothy L. Smith, *Revivalism and Social Reform: American Protestantism on the Eve of the Civil War* (Nashville: Harper & Row, 1957), 231–232.
2. Ibid., 177.
3. Ibid., 174.
4. Ibid., 163.
5. Ibid., 167.
6. Ibid., 169–173.
7. Ibid., ch. 10, "The Evangelical Origins of Social Christianity," esp. 151, 158, and 162.
8. The "great person" theory of leadership still holds popular sway but is not highly regarded in more recent discussions. See John Gardner's comments about "the balanced view" of the interplay between history and persons who emerge as leaders, in John W. Gardner, *On Leadership* (New York: The Free Press, 1990), 5–10. See also summary of the great man [sic] theories in Bernard M. Bass, *Bass and Stogdill's Handbook of Leadership: Theory, Research, and Managerial Applications*, 3d ed. (New York: The Free Press, 1990), 37–38, part of ch. 3, "An Introduction to Theories and Models of Leadership."
9. This distinction between leadership and management is widely understood in management literature. For a reference to it in a religious context, see Lovett H. Weems, Jr., *Church Leadership: Vision, Culture, Team, Integrity* (Nashville: Abingdon Press, 1993), 34–35.

CHAPTER 6

Edge of Somewhere

The Most Exciting Place for Ministry

EMPATHETIC MARGINALITY

Not Business as Usual

Finally, this great and terrible world war had ended and the nation was ready to get back to life again. Soldiers returned home from across the seas; gas rationing was phased out and automobile production resumed; girlfriends traded tear-stained letters for elated embraces and kisses; veterans headed off for college or a new job; wedding bells rang; hospitals filled with the cries of newborns; housing starts boomed. American citizens were eager to forget the pervasive struggles of the 1930s leading to the horror and tragedy of war. Things looked promising for the first time in years.

In the midst of all this, Gordon Cosby's musings on life after World War II ran somewhat differently than many. A Baptist preacher who had taken a leave of absence from his small congregation so that he could serve as a military chaplain, Cosby had been considering the challenges and opportunities of congregational ministry since his youth. He had been part of the Normandy invasion and received two Bronze Stars, but his heart felt heavy each time soldiers asked him their life-and-death questions. Even before the war had concluded, Cosby began to share in letters to his wife a vision for a church that would do what few churches ever had attempted: to establish an ecumenical congregation to overcome denominational divisions, to undertake "the spiritual reconstruction and rehabilitation" necessary to "take a world for Christ."

Once he returned home, Cosby and his wife set about working on this dream. The initial four persons grew to twelve by the time the fledgling congregation held its first official meeting, on October 5, 1946, in Alexandria, Virginia. The Rev. Mr. Cosby, however, had his sights set not on his native Virginia, but rather on the inner neighborhoods of the capital city a few miles away, Washington, D.C.[1]

Hardly two decades later, the Church of the Savior had become one of the most well-known congregations in the United States. Its School of Christian Living prepared prospective members with a rigorous series of study courses about the faith. Its primary facility was an old Victorian mansion on Massachusetts Avenue, but it also began and sustained various ministries in other locations. A 175-acre multi-purpose facility in nearby Maryland provided retreat space, an old farmhouse, a pond, fields, stables, a tree farm, vineyards, an orchard, an amphitheater, and other resources aimed at one overriding purpose: "to be a place where the lives of everybody who touched it could become more deeply rooted in the life of God."[2] Several members felt led to establish "The Potter's House," a coffee house where the diverse people of Washington, D.C., could come to discuss issues of the day in an atmosphere devoid of religious symbols but filled with the spirit of its congregation. They studied and prayed together regularly, in addition to arranging programs, serving coffee, and cleaning restrooms.

These and many other thriving ventures were undertaken by a congregation that never reached more than 140 members.[3] Each one of these persons completed all ten courses in the School of Christian Living and prepared a four-part statement of faith, including a commitment to the ministry tasks of the congregation.[4] Typically, worship attendance numbered many more than the membership itself. Pastors and believers from around the country and world considered a visit to Church of the Savior almost a pilgrimage of their faith. It looked like Church of the Savior had it made.

Choosing an Edge

Clearly, Church of the Savior is not a run-of-the-mill congregation. Its call to commitment interpreted the Christian faith in terms of high expectations of energy and time, yet in a low-key but clear manner. Church members were free to consider and propose various forms of ministry. Such ventures had to meet three criteria: to nurture those who are involved with it; to serve others in need, through suffering and sacrifice; and to spread the good news. Evangelism, however, was linked to the service itself: it was not to occur by words alone.[5] Through trial and error, struggle and accomplishment, Church of the Savior became a church to which many others looked for inspiration and insight about the nature of faith and commitment.

In many respects, Church of the Savior is a rare phenomenon. Its many achievements in ministry and service, undergirded and guided by its distinctive way of engaging member, visitor, and active nonmember alike, set it far apart from those much more familiar congregations where a good day is when one-half of the official membership shows up for worship—and nothing else. Church of the Savior is not for many who would profess the Christian faith. It is not big, or flashy, or dramatic, or on television; its pastor is not photogenic or charismatic; it is not located in an attractive suburb; it does not have a family life center or offer simple-sounding formulae for success in life. Instead, what this now-"scattered" congregation (more on that part of the story later) illustrates is perhaps one of the purest forms of the one contextual posture that we have yet to discuss in detail.

In this chapter, we learn more about empathetic marginality, the posture that I propose is the one most needed in the world today. Yet moving into empathetic marginality does not at all mean imitating a church that you think "has made it." Church of the Savior is rare also because the story of its founding and early years suggest that it began and maintained life in this posture of empathetic marginality. By contrast, almost all existing congregations today began out of one of the other three postures. Nonetheless, I urge you to resist the temptation to suppose that your church could be as effective in ministry by imitating Church of the Savior—or any other church you read about here or know of yourself. Instead, I encourage you to be instructed by their contrasts and distinctive ministries.

What we then discover in Church of the Savior is a congregation that chose and maintained life in faith on some kind of edge. Not only this, but its capacity for choosing was driven by a commitment to create a congregation that would be reaching out constantly. Thus, one of the key characteristics of empathetic marginality that Church of the Savior exhibits is a conscious choice about its stance with the world and its focus of identity. It is the kind of church in which, so to speak, lemonade gets in its blood.

General Characteristics

Besides their intentionality, empathetic marginal congregations display a few basic qualities in common. For one thing, *their rhythm of life seems pretty well balanced.* Energy within the membership does not get too concentrated in one or two areas of the church's life, as it tends to do with inner-directed conventionality. For churches in this latter posture, activities that revolve around reinforcing existing activities and networks of relationships tend to dominate. These could include a familiar, traditional worship service, auxiliaries, and Sunday School classes with few new members, and lots of attention given to the appearance and condition of the church facilities. In empathetic marginality, however, the congregation as a whole willingly spends time and energy in a number of ways. It considers its worship, nurture, fellowship, and service ministries all with equal care and importance; every ministry receives adequate resources.

One of the reasons for this kind of creative balance in empathetic marginality is, second, that these churches are *effective at articulating their edge.* Members know where the church locates itself in the world and how the church directs its attention. In many cases, this articulation becomes expressed in a formal "mission statement," in which the congregation declares its purpose and understanding of mission. For many other congregations, however, such statements are often hollow exercises. Empathetic marginal churches put into words what is deep in their conviction; the mission statement is not "the tail wagging the dog." Both pastors and church members talk about the nature of this edge of which the congregation has chosen to make something. These discussions continue to reaffirm clarity and commitment, as well as stimulate new thinking about how to sustain ministry from that edge.

A third quality among empathetic marginal churches is how *the expectations of membership are mirrored through the very balance of its activity.* Members tend not to "bunch up" in a few high-status groups or endeavors but spread out by interest to participate. This was quite the case with Church of the Savior. In their arrangement of things, membership was preceded by completing the School of Christian Living and succeeded by selecting a mission group in which to study, pray, and undertake some form of service. In other words, empathetic marginal churches seem to have more members who are active in more than one way. Commitment to the congregation's life and mission is taken seriously.

Fourth, empathetic marginal churches often belie a simple labeling as either *"conservative"* or *"liberal."* Some scholars of American religion already argue that these labels for churches

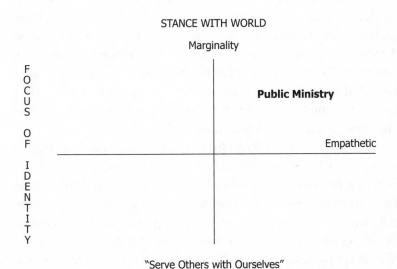

STANCE WITH WORLD

Marginality

FOCUS OF IDENTITY

Public Ministry

Empathetic

"Serve Others with Ourselves"
THE CHURCH ON THE EDGE OF SOMEWHERE

are less helpful today than they might have been in the past. Church of the Savior was founded by a Baptist preacher with a vision for evangelizing the whole world.[6] Yet, no one who worshiped with the congregation or participated in any of its many mission programs would have felt pressured with some ardent or clever plea to think and behave in a certain way. When a community of faith claims an edge in its world, it must learn to wrestle with all of the consequences. As our spiritual ancestor Jacob found out (Genesis 32:22–32), wrestling with God does not leave a person in an easily defined place.

A fifth, perhaps surprising, quality of empathetic marginal churches is that they tend to be *located in urban areas*. Why? Cities have abundant diversity and contrasts. Homeless white women can be seen walking on the same sidewalk as handsomely dressed black, white, and Asian men en route for their tall office buildings. One is just as likely to hear a symphony as rap music from passing cars. Cities are more cosmopolitan than towns; they have more different kinds of people, more contrasts of race, education, wealth, and opportunity; and they tend to be the places where all kinds of changes happen first. Cities also have a higher density of population; people live closer together than in farm country, the suburbs, or towns. Such proximity usually results in more contact of one kind or another with people who are different than you in some ways and like you in others. Consequently, churches in cities face more diversity and more rapid and extensive changes than do towns in northern Vermont or southern Utah. Thus, city churches have to come to terms with factors that they did not create and often cannot change. A few of those churches wrestle with the angel long enough to receive the blessing of claiming their marginality.

Sixth, unlike many other city churches, empathetic marginal congregations have both *developed and utilized access to sufficient and various resources*. Remember that "resources" are both material and human. One of the mistakes that inner-directed conventional churches can make is in assuming that having plenty of material resources (income, investments, property) guarantees ministry. Empathetic marginal churches have learned that human resources make the difference. These include formal education, vocational skills of all kinds, life experience, networks, relationships, and—this is key—the willingness to learn. A mountain of material resources without the will or ability to do something creative with them does not help a church pursue its gospel ministry. Empathetic marginal churches are very capable of using human resources in order to gain access to the material resources that their mission needs.

Finally, empathetic marginal churches tend to be *guided by a clearly articulated vision*. I have written expansively about the development and use of church vision elsewhere.[7] Here, suffice it to say that vision is a mental picture of the future that the congregation believes is its call from God. Not all congregations have visions like this; many of them do not. Even those who write a mission statement and vote on it have not necessarily created a vision or learned how to follow it. Churches in the posture of inner-directed conventionality usually do not have either vision or "a" vision. By contrast, churches in empathetic marginality recognize at least an implicit vision in their midst.

Why is vision so common among them? Consider the nature of this posture. It is difficult, if not impossible, to maintain the commitment and energy that keeps its empathy in tension with its marginality, unless the congregation looks beyond itself in some focused way. Otherwise, entropy will drag the congregation away from either its empathy or its marginality. To which direction it will retreat depends upon basic factors of the congregation's existence that are ascribed (given by the situation) rather than achieved (attained by their own accomplishments). We will elaborate upon this point a little later in this chapter.

Context: A Deeper Look

Two of the points above, concerning an urban setting and resource access, suggest that it would useful to pause a moment and think a bit more carefully about how congregational life and ministry are so profoundly influenced by context. Let me use myself as an illustration.

My capacity for analyzing, let alone understanding, a church's context was woefully inadequate when I graduated from seminary. Few of the courses in the curriculum focused at all on social, cultural, legal, economic, and political features of the world in which congregations find themselves. Today, I can hardly imagine thinking about any particular church without accounting for the characteristics—both obvious and subtle—of its surroundings. Similarly, empathetic marginal churches have become context-sensitive: they have found ways to recognize, interpret, and respond to the often shifting realities of life right outside their doors.

Yet, there is a dimension to context that might be easy to overlook, even though its effects upon life today are incontrovertible. Any category that can be used to analyze context has a *historical dimension* to it. What we in American society sometimes forget is that our way of life, historically speaking, is quite new to the scene. The political forms of democracy that we espouse and by which we order our government and society emerged in relatively recent times. To put it another way, the American experiment in democracy is only in its third century. Its economic partner throughout this experiment, capitalism, is also relatively new. An economy dominated by multinational "corporations" heavily dependent upon post-industrial technology is a far cry from villages where every family survives by growing its own food and trading some of it for other goods. Both of these dominant forms, political and economic, find their ancestry in particular developments primarily in Europe of the late middle ages and early modern period. Their current versions are so familiar to Americans that we easily forget how a couple of centuries is a short time for such dramatic shifts in economics and governance to occur.

Imagine what it might be like for congregations that live in a country ruled by a king or a dictator. In nations where the position at the head of the country makes all the rules, churches—like all other social and other groups in that country—exist at the whim of the king or dictator. There is no protection of law under which even the monarch must abide. Political strictures of this kind were the way of life for virtually all humans throughout most of history. Their effect on economic patterns could be, and often were, just as restrictive. The only people who accumulated wealth were the ruler and those whom the ruler allowed to accumulate wealth. Any form of religion, including a state church, thus existed at the favor of the ruler. Without any other forms of protection, the church at every level had to remain sufficiently in that ruler's good graces in order to do what it wanted. In most cases, church structures were considered an arm of the state.

It was not until the gradual changes that led medieval Europe into a different era that the concepts and social practices that Americans take for granted became possible. In the form of capitalistic democracy that the United States has created and promoted, people are free to associate and join together at their own will. This concept is often referred to as "voluntary association," and its expression in American life is so pervasive that we take it for granted. It encourages us to choose where we live, what we do for a living, where we spend our money and for what goods and services, and what organizations we might join. Church becomes one such organization. Clearly, in American history, churches have played a significant role in society, hardly a sideline, even as they have not always been allowed free association to determine their own members.

Still, it is clear from history that Americans today live with economic and political structures that encourage voluntary associations, including those such as churches.[8]

Political and economic factors are not the only kinds to affect congregational context, however. Another key element, subtle yet quite powerful, is *culture.* Think about the nation of Japan for a moment. It has a very long history and pride in its own accomplishments and distinctive culture. Since the end of World War II, Japan has engaged the international economy in dramatic and impressive ways. Its political structures have changed: the ancient monarchy, still revered, has become mostly ceremonial, while the nation's political structures and processes resemble Western forms. Even with its transformation to a world player, however, religion in Japan is very different than it is in the West or the United States in particular. Shrines of the ancient Shinto religion remain; Buddhist temples and monasteries also have long histories in Japan; Christians constitute only a small fraction of the nation's population.[9]

What do you think it is like for Christians in Japan? They do not live in a cultural context in which religion is viewed as highly voluntary in the same way that it is in the United States. In which contextual posture might the small minority of churches in Japan most easily find themselves? Toward which contextual posture might they seek to move, and for what reasons? What forms of social ministry and evangelism stand a chance of being effective? Would a church in Japan even measure "effectiveness" the same way Americans do, given American fascination with megachurches, large gatherings, and profitable marketing?

Any church needs to understand its context, with all of its complexity and subtlety, if it is to engage in ministry that is gospel-driven. May such awareness of context push and pull and call you to see the need for more churches in empathetic marginality.

Biblical and Theological Themes

A congregation that has made its way into the sweet struggle of ministry on the edge listens to the Bible and hears things that most other congregations do not hear. Their use of particular texts might vary, but their practice of theology will express a view of faith and life that resonates with certain kinds of texts. What are some of these?

In one way or another, empathetic marginal congregations hear their call to ministry in words from the prophetic traditions. The transition that we see in the contextual posture grid, inner-directed to empathetic, is suggested in some texts and quite apparent in others. In the Servant Song of Isaiah 49, this dual focus comes through quite dramatically. The LORD speaks to the servant in these words:

> [God] says,
> "It is too light a thing that you
> Should be my servant
> To raise up the tribes of Jacob
> And to restore the survivors of Israel;

> I will give you as a light to the nations,
> That my salvation may reach to
> The end of the earth." (Isaiah 49:6)

This prophet, reflecting on the fall of Jerusalem and exile in Babylon, does not take the logically easy path of merely reassuring the remnant of Israel that God will give it back its land, monarchy, and status as a nation-state. Such an action would be like a promise of inner-directed conventionality (return of their state) to a community living in inner-directed marginality (camps in exile). Instead, the prophet stretches the readers' perception of their life and promise with the LORD to the edge of its imagined credulity. "It is not enough," the prophetic voice utters, "to get back what you once possessed and enjoyed. God has more in mind for you. You have a purpose beyond yourselves. Those other peoples who inhabit the lands around you need the wholeness of life that I intend for all creatures. You will become like a beacon for them and for all peoples everywhere."

A mission this big does not allow a community of faith to crawl back into its own simple security. Empathetically marginal congregations take such a mission to heart, and yet it is tempered and channeled by other realities. These realities are whispered elsewhere in the Scriptures. Why should a faith community believe that the God who so cares for them would expect them to care so deeply for others? What is it about our biblical faith that could compel a church to embrace empathy with energy? The answer in the Bible, I suggest, is tucked away among texts that many earnest readers skip over, thinking that they are concerned with religious rules that do not apply anymore. The Book of Deuteronomy contains many such lists, filled with exhortations of behavior to undertake and to avoid. Among these lists, two of them hold the clue, the insight that drives the empathetically marginal church.

Both of these lists refer to a trio of categories in antiquity that functioned as code language for those who are vulnerable to oppression. This trio is variously listed, based on the translation, as "the sojourner, the fatherless, and the widow" or "the orphan, the widow, and the stranger/alien." In each one of the three cases, persons in the category were afforded few protections; they were the most likely to fall through the cracks of a social and legal system (does any of this sound familiar today?). In both the tenth and the twenty-fourth chapters of Deuteronomy, the newly settled Israelites are commanded to "execute justice," to "provide food and clothing," to allow aliens, widows and orphans to glean the fields after harvest (10:18; 24:17, 19–21; see also Exodus 22:21–22).

Why?

The answer is simple yet so profound: "because you know what it is like to be in their shoes."

How so?

"Because you were in Egypt; you were strangers and slaves there—and your LORD rescued you."

These texts appeal to *empathy*. The Israelites are being reminded that their existence relies solely upon the generosity of God on their behalf. The story of slavery in and escape from Egypt has become the pivotal memory of Israel's self-understanding. Indeed, the connection is even stronger, for love of God (in response to grace) is expressed through love for those who are "weakest and most disadvantaged."[10] Empathy grows out of rich, real-life experiences of being loved. Such experiences are not trite or contrived but emerge in congregations that seek to be responsible in their faithfulness.

These texts also appeal to *marginality*. Being slaves and sojourners in biblical times meant living right on the edge of security and comfort. The Deuteronomistic editor bore a keen sense that these theocratic laws would lose their vitality without continual attention to those vivid moments in Hebrew history where the action of God on their behalf was so very evident. In particular, God rescued them from oppression and then from certain death at the Red Sea. They know what it is like to be persecuted, to go wanting, to fear for their lives. It is as though these several texts are saying, "Remember your own marginality as you deal with those in your midst who themselves live marginally."

Of course, the theme of empathy moves even more clearly in the New Testament. We see, for instance, Jesus answering a Pharasaic lawyer that the greatest commandment has two parts—to love God fully and to love neighbor as oneself (Matthew 22:34:40). Yet, if we pay close attention to other New Testament passages, we will become aware also of the place that marginality played in the life of Jesus and the first followers. Jesus himself was raised in a remote, small town. The fourth Gospel reports that, when Philip told Nathanael about Jesus, Nathanael replied, "Can anything good come out of Nazareth?" (John 1:46). Nazareth was located in Galilee, in the northern part of the old kingdom, about a three days' journey from the capital city of Jerusalem. In anyone's estimation, it was not a highly regarded region. The day of Pentecost account in Acts 2 picks up on Galilee's less-than-stellar social status. In this account, "devout Jews from every nation under heaven living in Jerusalem" (2:5) heard Jesus' followers speaking about the wonders of God in the languages of their homelands (2:6). The writer of Acts reports that this listening crowd was "bewildered . . . amazed and astonished," and inquired aloud, "Are not all these who are speaking Galileans?" (2:7) In other words, they were country bumpkins, so "how could they have learned to speak our languages?"

The Christian movement clearly began as a marginal phenomenon. Just as some of the Jerusalem crowd "sneered" and attributed the disciples' behavior to inebriation (Acts 2:13), so also has some of the most faithful Christian witness in history been marginalized by social status and pressure. Unlike churches of the other three postures, what empathetic marginal congregations understand and embrace is that marginality never should be completely avoided or dismissed. "When life gives you lemons. . . ." These churches hear texts like those discussed above and interpret them as symbols of faith living on some kind of edge, a place to which they are led by God.

Cultural Dimensions

Yet simply agreeing in principle that the church will embrace biblical theology espousing empathy and marginality does not actually make a church empathetic and marginal. The congregation

learns to live into its call. It demonstrates its commitment in all of
its activities, programs, and ministries. It demonstrates a remarkable capacity for living with different sorts of tensions in a creative way. Empathetic marginal congregations tend to have a lot
going on, but their activity reveals an understanding of ministry
that is quite comprehensive. To an outsider, this array of activity
might not always appear to be congruent with itself. How does a
Bible study for seniors or a roller skating party for middle school
kids connect up in the church's life with a letter-writing ministry
to prisoners or a visit to city hall? The congregation's internal co-
herence, however, becomes more evident the more carefully one
observes. An empathetic marginal church does not let grass grow
under its feet. Decisions about what it does are not based merely
upon precedent or tradition but with studied consideration of
how the particular activity helps the congregation to fulfill its vision.[11] What we can observe of empathetic marginal churches is
their energy for ministry all across the board.

What we hear empathetic marginal churches say about what
is important to them could sound much like what we hear from
other congregations. Such statements usually express both identity and activity: "We are warm and friendly," "We are a big family," and others are common versions of these kinds of sayings.
Often, however, empathetic marginal churches find a way to
turn a creative corner, as they articulate their edge. One African
American pastor, for instance, stated in his annual report one year
to the congregation that he wanted them to be "Black, Christian,
and proud."[12] This pastor's emphasis became something of a ral-
lying cry for a congregation seeking to find its place and mission
in the wake of the civil rights movement. Empathetic marginal
churches have wrestled among themselves enough to be able to
speak in affirming as well as revealing terms about what they
value and seek.

Deep down inside of them, these cutting-edge churches hold
certain convictions that definitely go beyond the deep beliefs of
congregations in the other postures. For instance, I think that
many empathetic marginal churches are driven by a conviction
that *"If we fit into the world completely, we would lose our leverage*

for what we do." Churches in this posture, as I have said, do not arrive here by accident. They have dealt with the matters of both identity and world stance in such a way as to have embraced an honesty about themselves that many congregations never reach. This honesty helped to move them to live out of the edge that they now claim as essential for their ministry. As a result, empathetic marginal churches are much more likely to resist anything that feels like some manner of conformity.

Empathetic marginal churches also seem to have a healthy dose of realism. I think that another one of their underlying beliefs tends to be something like, *"The world is not necessarily good, but it can be changed for the better."* Neither too optimistic nor too pessimistic, empathetic marginal congregations seem deeply convinced that they are capable and motivated to address life's distresses in some way. They tend to believe that *"Anyone can make a difference,"* confident that individual persons can bring their resources to bear upon even difficult situations. A related belief in empathetic marginality seems often to be that *"All of human life, individual and collective, has value in and of itself."* Empathy tends to see and honor good and potential in others. These congregations are more likely to treat people who are different as partners in the ventures of life. When those partners suffer, empathetic marginal churches feel with those circumstances and reach out to do something about it.

What makes any congregation what it is are these underlying beliefs that they hardly ever discuss but which guide everything that they do.[13] In the case of empathetic marginality, these beliefs are quite consistent with the congregation's activity and its statements of value.

How Do You Get There from Here?

Empathetic marginality is a posture that can be entered from more than one of the other three postures. It seems highly unlikely that churches can become empathetic and marginal at the same time by moving directly out of inner-directed conventionality. One of the reasons for this sober assessment becomes evident by look-ing at the overall grid. Empathetic marginality does not overlap inner-directed conventionality on either part of its quadrants. This means that a church in the latter posture must make shifts in both of its basic positions; such a double-edged task is not impos-sible, just very difficult to pull off.

Since I estimate that at least half of all existing congregations today live out of inner-directed conventionality, this hypothesis should be cause for alarm. It implies that, although the need for empathetic marginality continues and grows, the largest bulk of existing congregations are not interested or ready to move in that direction. Self-absorption is a challenging inertia to overcome.

So, then, how can churches get to empathetic marginality? This is a key question, and we will explore it in more detail in the final chapter. For the purposes of this chapter, I will say that it is more likely to occur with congregations that already share one of its basic characteristics in their current posture. That is, they already are marginal or they already are empathetic: they are in inner-directed marginality or empathetic conventional-ity. Yet the plot thickens. Inner-directed marginal churches hope eventually to move out of the need to meet crisis challenges constantly. When they accomplish this, it is usually by entering more into the mainstream of its immediate world, rather than remaining on its edge. That is, they become conventional, at least relatively speaking. The relief of this degree of security and comfort usually will not lend itself either to revisiting marginal-ity or embracing empathy. Therefore, it seems more likely (but not necessarily any more desirable) that existing congregations will enter empathetic marginality through the posture of empa-thetic conventionality.

Nothing guarantees any such move, however. From the per-spective of this book, the ultimate challenge for empathetic con-ventional churches is to decide to be willing to live with some kind of marginality. Conventionality symbolizes a comfort level (on whatever terms appeal to the particular congregation) that is difficult to abandon. Put another way, it takes energy to claim an edge and remain there.

What It Might Look Like

Let us clarify this discussion by looking at some realistic examples. Most of us would tend to admire an empathetic conventional church: it offers a lot and it gives to its community in some noticeable and useful way. In the world of the early twenty-first century, many if not most of the modest ratio of congregations now in this posture would be European American, white, middle-class churches with sufficient resources and a heart to help. We could predict this phenomenon because of the United States' history and current demographics. The diagram at the end of chapter 5 represents a possible move to empathetic marginality. This is a move that I believe many congregations would fear to make, since for them it would feel like letting go of their social security. Economic and social standing are strong forces, especially in a society like ours that allows and even encourages "upward mobility." It is for this reason that white churches with empathy will struggle to move out of their conventionality. They can still be contributing to ministry in their community, but they are likely to shy away from the risks that would lead to creative achievements in ministry for the common good.

Ironically, Church of the Savior dramatically restructured itself in part because of this fear. In 1976, after three decades of a distinctive life and renowned ministry to the Washington, D.C. area, Church of the Savior was disbanded by its founder, Gordon Cosby. He announced one Sunday morning to the 140-member congregation that it was time to spin off. Cosby was concerned that 140 was too large of a number to maintain the capacity for the "deeper, covenanted commitment" which was its hallmark for ministry. So he told the members that they were cut loose from Church of the Savior. He encouraged them to start over, to develop fresh groups. What was the purpose that Cosby had in mind? It was empathetic—"to better address what they would discern were the pressing needs around them."[14] In other words, to create the energy for marginality, Cosby believed that Church of the Savior members needed to redefine themselves—literally.

Not many congregations of the few who have embraced the posture of empathetic marginality do so from the beginning. This is not to say that it is impossible, but—under our present American social, economic, and religious trends—it seems less likely. I do hope, however, that an increasing number of new churches will be founded with the kind of clarity and conviction that creates empathetic marginality early on. What the realization of this hope might do for Christian witness in America this century I explore in the final chapter.

It seems much more likely that, in contrast to Church of the Savior, congregations in empathetic marginality will arrive here by some other path through the grid. Many congregations begin somewhere other than where they end up later. A high percentage of all congregations seems to live in the posture of inner-directed conventionality. Some started out there, by virtue of being established in a context fairly compatible with the congregation's initial membership. Others began in marginality, reflecting the daunting odds for success that the congregation's clientele faced vis-à-vis its immediate world. As their members became more settled economically, those inner-directed churches move out of their initial marginality, into the higher status of conventionality. This section suggests that the particular forms of ethos that emerge with each contextual posture make some posture shifts more likely than others. We could expect, for instance, that a church in inner-directed marginality would seek the kind of stability that inner-directed conventionality represents. Conventionality appears to be the more likely half of the grid toward which to gravitate and remain.

Claiming and Reclaiming an Edge

The empathetically marginal church of Trinity United Church of Christ in Chicago presents a fascinating study of perhaps unexpected posture shifts. Its history tells of a congregation established for a distinctive purpose, which then was gradually replaced in the wake of major social transitions stimulated by the civil rights movement. Trinity was founded in 1961 by a majority-white denomination seeking to diversify its ethnic makeup. After hoping briefly that it could establish an integrated congregation with copastors who were black and white, the Chicago Metropolitan Association decided instead to found a church for middle-class blacks. Their assimilation into the denomination was anticipated to be much easier that way, which in retrospect led to some interesting contradictions. For instance, the congregation supported civil rights activity in the South instead of addressing the class divide between themselves and their housing project neighbors.[15]

Here are signs, then, of a young Trinity Church living out of empathetic conventionality—"empathetic" because of members' willingness to picket in support of the 1965 march to Selma; "conventional" because of the church's middle-class location and comfort. Several years later, however, a pastoral departure signaled Trinity's struggle with its identity and mission. Two-thirds of its members had left, leaving the congregation under 100 members. Their location on the South Side of Chicago had changed racial composition rapidly: few neighborhoods remained with a significant white population. The Black Power movement was active in their area; Dr. King had been assassinated; college protests over civil rights and the Vietnam war were subsiding. In the space of just one decade, the demographic and social conditions that supported Trinity's original mission had shifted dramatically. Trinity's interim pastor helped the church's members talk about what was going on around them and inside them.

As a result of these conversations, the pulpit committee adopted a statement that would point the congregation in a different direction. It was committing the church to "confronting, transforming, and eliminating those things in our culture that lead to the dehumanization of persons and tend to perpetuate their psychological enslavement."[16] With this statement as its guide, the pulpit committee identified one pastoral candidate whose answers in their interview excited them: the Rev. Dr. Jeremiah Wright. He began his pastorate at Trinity aware that the congregation was nervous about what this new focus would do to their status as middle-class folks who fit in. It took several years of working through changes in music and worship before the momentum turned favorably to reflect black consciousness.[17]

Fifteen years after Wright's installation as Trinity's pastor, the congregation had more than 4,000 members. Its worship service and music was transformed into a clear celebration of being "unapologetically black and unashamedly Christian." It had developed an extensive and innovative Christian education program that offered a variety of courses of all kinds for all ages in various settings.[18] Members had been given training and responsibilities to teach and to lead in all aspects of the congregation's life. Dr. Wright became active in denominational organizations dealing with race and justice, leading even to judicial involvements with legal cases that drew national attention.[19] Later, Trinity transformed its education ministries to an explicitly Africentric emphasis, including lectures and presentations by black scholars doing Africentric research and increased contact between Africa and nations of the African Diaspora.[20] The congregation has maintained a membership of 8,000 for a period of years, and more than 50 of them have gone on to graduate theological training.

The Power of an Edge

Trinity's story is remarkable in many ways. For one thing, it reveals how a congregation can shift from a conventional posture to empathetic marginality. The church realized that its context had changed dramatically since its inception, so it courageously redirected its focus, articulating a fresh vision. With leadership from its new pastor, Trinity began to make changes in order to fulfill that vision. The story of those changes and their consequences is not without struggle, however: three times in the first decade of Dr. Wright's ministry, a contingent of members left the church for other congregations. In the first case, those who left made up one-fourth of the original membership who extended their pastor his call. Not many years later, another contingent left and joined one particular congregation.[21] Trinity's experience in this matter illustrates that major change in any organization, even a church, sometimes cannot continue unless "cultural carriers" leave.[22] These are not situations to face glibly or callously, for the way that any disagreement is handled has an effect on the congregation in its future.

Trinity's shift to embracing its African identity and heritage was the key to its becoming a congregation in marginality. Because few churches anywhere in the United States at the time were moving in this direction, Trinity's decision required significant courage for taking risks. One of these risks was jeopardizing relationships with the denominational officials who had originally had a different kind of church in mind. Some tensions did arise at one point,[23] and probably others were less public, but Trinity has managed to navigate them with integrity. Dr. Wright's initiative and style all along have set a tone for pursuing Trinity's vision, evaluating its progress, developing new ministries—while staying true to what creates its edge.

A comparison of Church of the Savior and Trinity UCC helps us to realize that empathetic marginality is no cookie cutter stance. What creates the combination of marginality with empathy can, will, and should vary from congregation to congregation. A church started by educated, middle-class whites will find an edge that looks and feels different than a church that first defined itself as middle class and black before discerning a new vision in a new world. These two congregations can be contrasted in many ways, but we will miss the power of what they have in common if we focus on details of race, size, or location. For it is their commitment to pursue some significant edge within the context of their world (marginality), and to take the energy generated from being there and move it out into the very world from which it distinguishes itself (empathy) that is the important element they have in common.

What creates the drive for both empathy and marginality is a wrestling with what both Gordon Cosby and Jeremiah Wright see as central to the challenge of the gospel. As Cosby put it once, summarizing one of his themes since 1947, "the gospel is countercultural and unless we stand up against the prevailing culture we are just like that salt that has lost its flavor."[24] Cosby is very clear that he sees the source of this countercultural edge in Jesus himself: "Jesus wasn't crucified because he fed the multitudes and cured the lepers. He was crucified because he was questioning the temple, the status quo, the way things were."[25] Many Christians and congregations find this discovery too uncomfortable. On the other hand, empathetic marginal churches claim this point as the heart of their gospel ministry.

Leading from the Edge

What, then, does it take to sustain these kinds of churches, to keep up the commitment to live with empathy on an edge? In the case of empathetic marginality, leadership is an even more appropriate notion to apply, since this posture relies so heavily upon clarity of vision. Let us then consider five points, some of which have been implied already.

First, churches in empathetic marginality *empower their members to engage in ministry and equip them for their tasks.* Church of the Savior required everyone who joined to complete ten courses in its School of Christian Living. This period of study provided participants with a strong foundation in the nature of Christian faith and life. Then, when they joined the congregation, they were required also to become part of a mission group, which met regularly for study and prayer, to strengthen their work in mission. These two basic but demanding elements allowed members to be prepared to handle the challenges of ministry, knowing that they in a sense had been set free to put their faith into action.

Second, leadership in empathetic marginality *celebrates faith and achievement in the midst of embraced tensions.* The congregation learns that it has to have ways to live with and through the struggles that they have agreed to accept because of their mission. Sunday worship is one of the ways that Trinity UCC accomplishes this need. It is well known that African American church worship freely expresses a much more upbeat and affirming tone than the typical, traditional European American worship service. No matter what has happened during the week, an African American can go to church knowing that worship will lift her up, that she will "still be standing!" In this regard, Trinity is no different. Its worship, however, weaves together the strands of its empathy and its marginality in dramatic and uplifting ways. Here, worship does not provide an escape from the congregation's vision of mission, but rather a rehearsal of and empowering for it.

Third, to lead a church in empathetic marginality means to *teach the congregation how to identify and accept risk*. In a sense, it becomes second nature that risk of one kind or another is present in the life of these congregations. One thing that makes a difference, however, is that members, committees, staff, and others learn how to be clear about what kinds of chances they are taking. Elizabeth O'Connor tells the story of the many months of discussion, prayer, study, and preparation that went into Church of the Savior's decision in the late 1950s to open a coffee house.[26] So much work was necessary and there were no guarantees; the process from first conversation to opening day took two whole years. Yet, the Potter's House became a significant ministry of presence and outreach for Church of the Savior. "Calculated risk" is part of the equation in empathetic marginality of making decisions and implementing them.

A fourth way that leadership is exhibited in empathetic marginality occurs as the congregation *thinks theologically and articulates its understanding of the gospel in as wide-ranging terms as possible*. Whatever the congregation's analysis about its context, its place in that world, and the needs that it seeks to address, ultimately its discourse frames things in God-talk. Empathetic marginal congregations can think big and imagine big because of the way that they bring life-as-it-is into a deep conversation with the good news. Part of this process yields clarity about the church's vision, to be sure. Yet theological dialogue is not compartmentalized for these churches. Such conversation becomes part of the rhythm of its life, not as glib recitation of slogans, but as exploration, articulation, and affirmation. It is one significant way to maintain the energy of this challenging but rewarding posture.

The other side of this conversation always must be, of course, the congregation's present (not desired or imagined) stance toward the world. Marginality by nature pushes back and does not make it easy for the congregation to remain there.

Fifth and finally, empathetic marginal churches *continue to discuss the nature of their own marginality*. They cannot afford to take their edge for granted, because their world does not do so and thus can misunderstand it easily. Part of the challenge for these churches is the energy it takes to interpret the church to its world (and to other churches!). Not only this, but as the world itself changes, one marginal position might evolve into a conventional one, thus taking the church away from its edge. One never knows what kind of lemons will appear. If a congregation in empathetic marginality allows its cadence of intentional reflection to wither, it is in danger of losing its marginality—and perhaps also its empathy.

How to Find an Edge

In this chapter, I have described what I consider to be the church of the future. Most of us are not there, and whether we can help our churches get there remains to be seen. I am cautiously optimistic but only as I am convinced that, eventually, enough churches will be left standing to realize that they cannot keep up business as usual. How can the vast majority of churches that are not on an edge find one out of which to do ministry? This is the primary question for our final chapter.

Notes

1. Story details in this and the previous paragraph come from Elizabeth O'Connor, *Call to Commitment* (New York: Harper & Row, 1963), 7–17.
2. Ibid., 57.
3. Paul Wilkes, *Excellent Protestant Congregations: The Guide to Best Places and Practices* (Louisville: Westminster John Knox Press, 2001), 22.
4. O'Connor, op. cit., 29–30.
5. Ibid., 42–43.
6. See Diana Butler Bass, *The Practicing Congregation: Imagining a New Old Church* (Herndon, VA: The Alban Institute, 2004), 69–76.
7. *Futuring Your Church: Finding Your Vision and Making It Work* (Cleveland: The Pilgrim Press, 1999). See also my article, "Leader-

ship for Congregational Vitality: Paradigmatic Explorations into Open Systems Organizational Culture Theory," *Journal of Religious Leadership,* Vol. 2, No. 1, Spring 2003, 53–86.

8. For a helpful exploration of the concept of voluntary associations, see James Luther Adams, *Voluntary Associations: Socio-Cultural Analyses and Theological Interpretation* (Chicago: Exploration Press, 1986), esp. ch. 10, "The Voluntary Principle in the Forming of American Religion."

9. Basic information about religion in Japan is easily accessed on several websites, such as www.web-japan.org/factsheet/religion/today.html and www.aisaninfo.org/asianinfo/japan/religion.htm. Both of these Web sites were accessed for this book on 29 December 2006.

10. Walter Brueggemann, *Theology of the Old Testament: Testimony, Dispute, Advocacy* (Minneapolis: Fortress Press, 1997), 422; see also 460, 305, and 240.

10. For a discussion of applying an articulated congregational vision to its decision-making processes, see my *Futuring Your Church: Finding Your Vision and Making It Work* (Cleveland: The Pilgrim Press, 1999), ch. 6, "Moving Ahead—Making Your Vision Work," and ch. 7, "On Not Losing Heart—The Perils and Promises of Futuring."

12. Julia Speller, *Walkin' the Talk: Keepin' the Faith in Africentric Congregations* (Cleveland: The Pilgrim Press, 2005), 86.

13. For an extensive discussion of the influence of these underlying beliefs as the foundation of an organization's culture, see Edgar Schein, *The Corporate Culture Survival Guide: Sense and Nonsense about Culture Change* (San Francisco: Jossey-Bass, 1999), chs. 3 and 4, esp. 15–19 and 48–87.

14. Wilkes, op.cit.

15. Speller, op.cit., 74–77.

16. Ibid., 80–81.

17. Ibid., 81–84.

18. Ibid., 85.

19. Ibid., 87–88.

20. Ibid., 92–95.

21. Ibid., 89.

22. Schein, op.cit., 168.
23. Speller, op.cit., 90.
24. Wilkes, op.cit., 36.
25. Ibid., 37.
26. O'Connor, op.cit., ch. 9.

CHAPTER 7

Finding Your "Edge of Somewhere"

Leadership and the Church of the Twenty-First Century

The Vitality of Living on an Edge

In the previous chapter we looked at Church of the Savior in Washington, D.C. It is a very unusual congregation in many respects. Perhaps first of all, it was founded as a nondenominational church in an era in which denominations dominated the American religious scene. It then deliberately located itself, not in a neighborhood where "people like us" lived, but in a neglected and struggling community with many problems and needs. The congregation never built a church facility, but purchased existing buildings and modified them for their purposes. Church of the Savior also chose to expect specific kinds of things from those who became official members—ten courses of schooling, a pledge of resources, and selection of a particular mission group for prayer, study, and action. Although many people have worshipped over the years with Church of the Savior, its membership never grew larger than 140. If all these characteristics were not unusual enough, Church of the Savior did something else that few congregations ever do: it "scattered" itself. After three decades of noteworthy and distinctive life and mission, the congregation broke up into several smaller groups. Each one decided to focus upon one specific form of mission, as those of similar interest identified those forms.

It has been six decades since Church of the Savior held its first worship service and began the kind of Christian witness that has become its hallmark. What has happened to it over these years of great economic, social, cultural, and international changes? Is it possible for a congregation like Church of the Savior to survive and even sustain the original spirit of its distinguishing purpose?

A Pilgrimage

Not long before finishing the manuscript for this book, my wife Beverly and I were in Washington, D.C., and had an opportunity to check in on Church of the Savior. Years ago in seminary, I had attended a retreat led by two of the church's members. I had gone to the retreat with great anticipation, having read in college church member Elizabeth O'Connor's books about Church of the Savior.[1] These stories and reflections on Christian witness both fascinated and puzzled me. Having grown up in a church that in retrospect seemed quite inner-directed and conventional, I felt a deep attraction to the level of commitment and accomplishment that O'Connor portrayed. The closest that I had ever come to such an experience were the student praise-and-prayer groups that I had attended and led during my college years. None of us, however, had been living out in the world of work, juggling a job, career, family, church, and all the rest. What did it actually look like to be a member of Church of the Savior? This question remained in the back of my mind for many years. Now, in Washington, D.C., and discovering that the church was still open and in walking distance, I had a different question: has this church been able to keep its vision and mission alive? Can a congregation that moved so quickly into empathetic marginality sustain itself, in spite of a world of fast-moving changes?

Beverly and I walked up Massachusetts Avenue on a cloudy but dry Sunday morning. I realized how much anticipation and wonder was inside of me during the moments when we crossed DuPont Circle and entered the block where the church is located. We were almost right in front of the classic three-story brownstone structure before I saw the brass-plated sign next to the front door that reads, "Church of the Savior." The sign holds onto the stones through a thin, weathered piece of lumber. Here and there, I noticed patches of tuckpointing between certain stones. A passerby easily could mistake the small old mansion for an abandoned building. Beverly thought that it was empty, but we walked up the granite-slab steps anyway and tried the door knob. When it opened, we saw a light or two around to the right and heard low voices. We entered the foyer, and our brief pilgrimage took its next step.

In my experience as a pastor, I have sensed that many people these days who go to church still want something that "looks like" church. The megachurch, spare-of-religious-symbols trend aside, there are still a lot of us who seek a space that feels sacred in part because of its look and feel. Church of the Savior's building, its original purchase, surely had been built by a well-to-do person, but it was no church structure. I love poking around old stylish homes like this one, so it felt a bit out of context to me to see the original woodwork, windows, staircases, and stonework and remind myself that this "house" had been used for sixty years as a gathering place for Christian worship and witness. The original grandeur of the first floor's main room has been muted by decades of modest but adequate (for Church of the Savior's purposes) maintenance. Hallways and doors seemed to turn every direction; stairways appeared from nowhere. Folding chairs were neatly lined up in the middle of the main room, providing seating for perhaps two dozen people.

Before we could begin to figure out where the sanctuary might be located, Beverly and I were greeted by several persons. At first, all of them were middle-aged and older, but by the time worship began, younger adults and a couple of teenagers came in, too. In our conversations, we felt neither politely tolerated nor desperately grabbed. One of my questions was whether Gordon Cosby, the church's founding pastor, was still alive. I did not have to figure out a polite way to ask this question, since a woman speaking with us turned to look at the bottom staircase steps and said rather casually, "Oh, here's Gordon now." Beverly and I agreed later that meeting Gordon Cosby was one of the unexpected highlights of our visit. At 89 years of age, Rev. Cosby is still very active and continues to preach regularly. He spoke to us with what I took to be a genuine interest and, later, remembered our names, hometown, and other details.

Understated

Church of the Savior worships in the old ballroom that it extended ten feet to accommodate more worshippers. It is a plain and simple room, long and somewhat narrow, with rows of chairs on either end facing each other. A piano sits on the street side of the long room. Opposite the double-door entrance stands the solid wooden lectern that Rev. Cosby uses for a pulpit. Behind this is a simple, carved wooden communion table, above which was the only object in the makeshift sanctuary that could be called artistic. It is a wooden cross, unevenly shaped, with the spaces between the crossbars filled with copper squares etched with photographs. The pictures tell the stories of many of Church of the Savior's ministry and mission activities. Beverly was overwhelmed by its beauty and symbolism.

In the minutes before worship commenced, several pieces of music were played through a sound system. Some of them sounded quite traditional and others were hauntingly spiritual in their style. We sang two hymns and used a printed bulletin for following the liturgy and reading announcements. Congregational prayer began with sharing of joys and concerns by anyone who chose to mention something. It was the Sunday before Thanksgiving, and Rev. Cosby spoke on "From Dullness and Duty to Joy." His words and line of thought were at once philosophical, theological, inspirational, and practical. He urged us to live daily out of joy rather than a sense of obligation. His closing story was a touching account of the unexpected wonder of connecting with other people when we give ourselves to our vocations gratefully.

More than half an hour passed from the time that worship ended and when Beverly and I finally left the building. Further conversations had ensued, further sharing of stories and interests opened us up, a brush with greatness slipped past us (Marian Wright Edelman, founder of the Children's Defense Fund, hugged Rev. Cosby before she left), and we left with commitments to stay in touch. The two of us talked about our visit all the way back to our hotel. I felt something like Cleopas and his friend must have felt with their unexpected hospitality toward the risen Lord on the road to Emmaus: "Were not our hearts burning within us while he was talking to us on the road, while he was opening the scriptures to us (Luke 24:32)?" We had heard a little, but just enough, about the ten "scattered" congregations of Church of the Savior to be confident that this congregation is still alive and well.

A History of the Future

The church on "the edge of somewhere" is the church of the future.

Church of the Savior is one congregation that seems to have maintained over the decades its ability to remain both marginal and empathetic. In America, churches in each one of the other three contextual postures will continue to exist, and some of them will contribute to gospel ministry. Others will survive but do little more than provide chaplaincy services for a shrinking group of longtime church members who probably never caught much of a glimpse of the biblical call anyway.

We have thought a great deal in this book about the grid and its four contextual postures, and yet there remain matters worth a bit more reflection. What are some of the primary implications of this model's insights about today's congregations and the challenges to live out of empathetic marginality?

I am not promoting a simple answer to the complex dynamics of church presence in a postmodern, shrinking world that both expresses and departs from American practices and values. In a sense, I seek the opposite—namely, that the reader will appreciate in this promise of empathetic marginality a way in which various forms of complexity can emerge constructively. This goal is informed in part by historical studies that point out how Protestant churches in the 1840s and 1850s, fueled by revival, left American society with influences far beyond their sheer numbers.[2] We noted how this revival was possible because of the churches' freedom to assemble and support themselves,[3] rather than function as a state church. We observed the historian's insight that this distinctive era brought about a blend of evangelical piety with a "more liberal social ethic".[4] We considered the shift during this era of social reform away from clergy domination to active initiative and leadership from laity, including women.[5] We also heard that theological seminaries redesigned their degree programs in order to emphasize sociology as a tool for ministry.[6]

History provides instructive lessons, if we listen to them. As the classic sociologist Max Weber pointed out, religious movements eventually become institutionalized,[7] and American religious history certainly exemplifies Weber's observation. As the United States was being born, three denominations dominated the colonial religious scene: Congregationalists, Presbyterians, and Episcopalians. These three all were fairly early in arriving among the North American English colonies and within a few generations becoming comfortable and secure in respective regions. By 1850, however, the largest denomination in the United States was none of these three but rather Methodism, a much later arrival. The Methodist churches had accomplished this rather remarkable feat with fewer educated clergy and modest material resources, but spurred on by a zeal that had not significantly waned. Another fifty years later, the Methodist Episcopal Churches in the United States had become proud of their higher clergy salaries, building construction, and pipe organs.[8] To a large extent, then, Methodism had lost its edge in society, joining instead the conventionality of the center of economic and social life.

Such patterns appear almost invariable, regardless of denomination. What they suggest for our purposes is that both congregational and denominational movement from one contextual posture to another is common—especially from inner-directed marginality to inner-directed conventionality. It took a revival like the one in the 1840s to stimulate among many well-established denominational congregations the kind of deeper interest for the world immediately around them. While certainly not every congregation or church body approved of revival theology and behavior,[9] those congregations and new organizations that did so also were likely to engage in some form of aid to needy populations. We reviewed this story at the beginning of chapter 5. The evidence from the early nineteenth century points to a general shift from inner-directed marginality (as with many Methodist churches) or inner-directed conventionality (as with many Presbyterian, Episcopalian, Congregational, and other well-established denominational congregations) to empathetic conventionality.

Similar patterns have continued in American religious history. The challenges they present to churches in the next few generations to some extent can be predicted, using the contextual posture grid. What sorts of dynamics would be involved?

Possible Congregational Paths

For instance, I mentioned in chapter 2 that the degree of strength for any posture is relative, not pure. That is, a congregation could be closer or farther away from the "boundaries" separating one posture from another. This observation recognizes how congregations are complex organizations, and one subculture—although dominant—does not necessarily represent everything about that congregation's life. An inner-directed conventional congregation could include a cadre of people whose commitment is to that church but whose spiritual interests center around serving others. This cadre could get involved with a homeless ministry, with mentoring at-risk children, or with some other activity aimed at improving the lives of marginal persons or groups. In such a scenario, the cadre is functioning as "empathetic" even though it is part of an "inner-directed" church. As time goes by, their activity could help move the entire congregation toward a stronger commitment to mission, which then would shift its posture. The grid, then, appears static but actually functions more as a snapshot in time. It is possible, and likely, that most congregations over the years are moving within the quadrant of one posture and then eventually into another posture.

Recognizing a church's fluidity among the postures leads also to the question of *patterns of movement*. What patterns are there from one posture to another that become fairly predictable? Two such patterns seem to explain the general histories of many American congregations. One of the patterns begins with churches in inner-directed marginality moving eventually to inner-directed conventionality (see positions 1 and 2 in the diagram below). As we saw at the end of chapter 3, inner-directed marginality is difficult to sustain indefinitely. It seeks some measure of stability, which it will achieve as it moves onto the conventional side of the grid. For such churches, however, the deeper question of faith is whether in some significant way their hearts can open to others. If they can, such churches are on their way to the empathetic quadrant of the conventional side. The history of American Methodism suggests that this pattern of movement between three of the four postures occurred for some congregations in the nineteenth and early twentieth centuries.[10] Lord Jesus Church's story, summarized in chapter 4, shows how difficult it can be to make the move to empathy.

A second, but less common, pattern of movement in the grid stays confined within the conventional side of the grid, from inner-directed to empathetic (see the diagram on the next page).

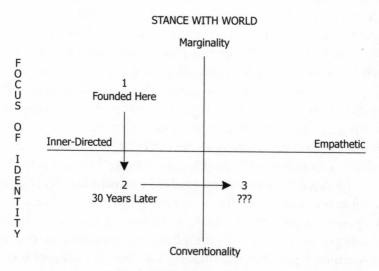

A COMMON PATTERN OF "POSTURE MOVEMENT"

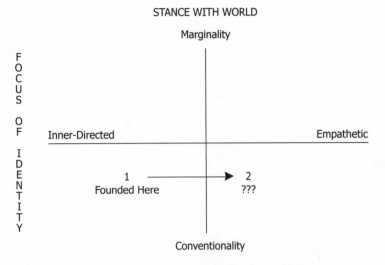

This pattern appears in congregations with no early experience of marginiality, since they were founded in a context in which they fit right in. We would expect many Congregational churches in New England, many Episcopal churches in Virginia, and certain Presbyterian congregations in North and South Carolina to have begun in inner-directed conventionality. As the decades went by, the challenge for such congregations would have been to develop genuine empathy, as their communities became more complex.

Churches in inner-directed conventionality are not likely to be pushed, however; the inertia of social and cultural security in one's own immediate environment is quite strong. If the congregation continues to feel satisfied with its life, it will tend to pursue what is familiar and comfortable. For long periods of time, American demographic patterns would have maintained the general trends that supported the stability of many Protestant congregations. The most recent example probably would be suburban churches in the 1950s that were founded before 1940. Population and economic booms in that era provided most of these congregations with all the fuel they needed to prosper materially. No wonder, then, that most of them could not empathize with prophetic voices emanating in the 1960s from a culturally distant urban setting.

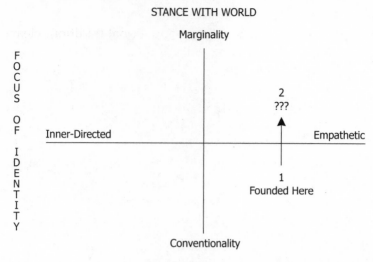

STANCE WITH WORLD

Marginality

F
O
C
U
S

O
F

I
D
E
N
T
I
T
Y

Inner-Directed

2
???

Empathetic

1
Founded Here

Conventionality

THE EMPATHETIC MOVE (IF IT HAPPENS)

Third, an even less likely move within the contextual posture grid begins in empathetic conventionality and crosses the line into marginality (see diagram above). By now you probably understand why such a move does not occur very often. For one thing, there are not that many churches in empathetic conventionality. In times of social upheaval, like those of the civil rights movement and the Vietnam war, however, the context of most congregations gets challenged. "Business as usual" is challenged along many fronts. Unsettling conditions in the wider society create perhaps the most likely opportunities for churches to move toward empathy and/or marginality. We probably could find in the early stories of both Church of the Savior and Trinity United Church of Christ persuasive evidence of moving from empathetic conventionality to empathetic marginality.

The Sociology of Grid Movement

Thinking about our congregations in terms of the contextual posture grid also reminds us of some of the sociological realities even within communities of faith. In reflecting upon extensive research about trends and patterns in late-twentieth-century

American mainline Protestantism, Kirk Hadaway and David Roozen argue that these several denominational traditions clearly have declined but can be revitalized. Part of their argument draws upon the Weberian distinction that we noted earlier between "movement" and "institution." Religious movements can grow quickly, until they gradually establish their own routines (Weber called it "routinization of charisma"). Once this happens, even the most zealous of religious movements settles in, acting more like an institution. At this point, Hadaway and Roozen argue, churches that were on the move now have become "captive to the demographic trajectories of their constituencies."[11] What is needed, therefore, to recover authentic energy again is a return to the sociological dynamics of a movement.[12] Essential to regaining such a movement-like quality, they continue, is not imitating other churches that currently are enjoying numerical growth, but rather getting clear about who they are and what they are called to become: "The key is a strong sense of identity and a compelling vision."[13]

For our purposes, the implications of Hadaway and Roozen's claims for revitalized American mainline denominations become even more pointed. For one thing, they argue further that the social and cultural conditions that supported "mainline" denominations in the first place have disappeared.[14] Instead, these two sociologists see strong opportunities for creating movements that give new shape to current cultural realities, putting a spin on what we already experience. The vision that redefines and reinterprets the church's life and role drives the transformation, even as new routines are established. At the same time, these routines, and the process of channeling a new movement, do not have to lead to cultural accommodation.[15]

Although Hadaway and Roozen are speaking specifically here of denominations, the assertions summarized here can apply just as powerfully to any one congregation. Conventionality eventually leads to stagnation and decline; any congregation is subject to the stability and also threatening inertia of becoming institutionalized. It can overcome this decline by choosing to become flexible again, to become movement-like. This intentional process is driven by vision that helps the church's members and constituents understand its identity and purpose, in light of its new context. That vision clarifies the congregation's relationship to its society in a fresh way. In the language of this book, a revitalized congregation is more likely to be moving into empathy and probably closer to marginality. Empathy might characterize the first part of this renewal move, but soon enough the environment will challenge the congregation to find its own edge. It is in moving to and maintaining the combination of empathy and marginality that the congregation faces its greatest trial.

Cultural Elements of "Stance toward World"

Though empathetic marginality is needed more than ever in today's world, it is a posture that is not easily attained. Discussions in chapters 5 and 6 have explained why marginality is a side of the grid from which most congregations seek to move away. Without sufficient conversation based on attention to context, no community of faith will choose to stay marginal. However, getting a handle on tools to analyze context becomes one step in a process of discovery and deliberate decision. Context relates to the congregation's "stance toward world" on the grid. One helpful way to understand context is by looking at it culturally, and one form of cultural measurement is by "scale." I call such scales "streams of culture" and they appear in several ways.[16] Analyzing how each of these streams is present in and around one's congregation helps to distinguish ways in which it can live out of marginality.

Streaming
A brief description of these categories of cultural streams will illustrate this potential. Every congregation has its own distinct culture, based on its own history and experience. At the same time, the sources for the particular configuration of the church's culture exist primarily outside of it. That is, congregational ethos does not appear out of nothing. It is most directly affected by its immediate surroundings, consisting of geography, climate, businesses, industry, occupations, ethnic groups, and many other

measurable factors that constitute its community. This scale is small, or "micro," with its own particular identity and cultural character. Yet it also is influenced by cultural streams beyond itself. One of those other streams is the large-scale, national character of the United States. As a nation, the United States has its own history of places, people, events, customs and the like. These represent the culture that has formed—and continues to adapt—over the decades and centuries. One way to understand the influence of this scale of "macro-" culture is to note that it affects everyone who lives or visits the country, whether they understand it, like it, fit in with it—or not.

In between the small and large streams of culture live several others. They are "meso-cultures," because their presence and influence is being considered from their location "in the middle." For instance, a person who grows up in New England will discover on a move to the South certain behaviors, values, and deep beliefs that are different. Such differences are based in distinctive elements of the two different regions of the country. Similarly, a Navajo woman who marries a man from Jamaica and settles with him in Atlanta will experience not only regional differences but racial/ethnic ones as well. People who are raised with material affluence live differently than those raised in poverty, but these differences extend beyond possessions and opportunity: they also include widely varying differences between the two social groups in their underlying assumptions about life. These brief examples point to levels of culture that flow through both American macroculture and all the thousands of microcultures that exist in the United States.

New Insight

Learning to analyze your congregation's context in cultural terms becomes a fascinating, complicated, yet very rewarding enterprise. You learn to pay attention to cues and clues that can be subtle but very strong. Gradually, you and your church realize how complex is your context, that part of the world which walks by and meets you at your church's front and back doors. You begin to see how many of the cultural elements in your church and in your neighborhood flow together to create unique combinations—even when those are not well understood. As you come to understand them, your church is more capable of navigating through their complexity. The congregation learns how to make decisions based on what it knows of itself and its community, rather than trying to meet some identified need by imitating a "successful" church.

Even more important in the long run, doing your own cultural analysis puts you in a stronger position for moving toward an edge. It takes serious and often somewhat uncomfortable congregational rumination to face what you discover about "who you are" in light of "where you are." The decision to live *with* marginality, or even to live *in* it, will not come easily. Cultural analysis becomes your ally in describing the cultural confluence that affects your church, as well as acknowledging its place on the contextual posture grid. Even at that, the truth does not necessarily set us free, if we do not want to receive it. Resistance to change often is rooted in denial of the truth. Your congregation likely will need to prepare for this kind of truth-telling and truth-accepting,[17] before it ever can feel the need to deal with marginality.

Two Ways of Approaching Your Edge

This discussion of cultural analysis also implies something about marginality that we have mentioned earlier. Not every congregation comes to marginality the same way. Hence, not every congregation will make marginality their "edge of somewhere" in the same way. The grid in this book suggests two basic ways in which churches find an edge, but they rarely get to choose which way. Understanding why this is so makes a big difference to the respective churches and their ministry.

As we noted in chapter 3, some congregations have no choice but to begin their existence in marginality. In these cases, however, their form of marginality almost always focuses upon the congregation as a community of security and support for a constituency living in stress. Economic and social conditions work against such constituencies, who in American history often were of an ethnic minority not favored by contemporary attitudes and behaviors. Groups with African, Italian, Irish, Asian, and native tribal heritage have suffered in American life simply because of their ethnic origins. Christian churches founded among these groups thus also are marginalized in society. This is their "ascribed" status—without a choice.

Out of Marginality

In American society, racial/ethnic communities still live with this legacy of marginality. In order to turn this ascribed status into an edge of somewhere, the churches in any of these communities must discover and embrace a way to live *through* it. In chapter 6 we met one congregation that has done this well for many years—Trinity United Church of Christ in Chicago. This congregation's testimony is far from acquiescent! Living with or through one's marginality does not mean pretending it is not there, or not important, or not at times hurtful. Rather, it means to acknowledge its reality and full characteristics, but to do so resourcefully rather than reactively. It means drawing upon the group's given status as a source of energy for Christian life and witness.

Race and ethnicity, while understandably being major categories for social and economic marginality, do not cover all forms of marginality. Any quality or characteristic that society as a whole considers less than fully acceptable can and does ascribe certain groups of people to marginal status. Yet, not all status is ascribed. In the modern era, another form of status emerged to become part of the American (macrocultural) myth: *achieved* status, or that form of communal regard based upon what a person or group has accomplished by virtue of accumulating education, wealth, or some other particular attainment. This form of status was exemplified in the Horatio Alger novels, in which a young man "pulls himself up by his bootstraps" through hard work and a lucky break here and there. The promise of "the American dream" continues the Alger metaphor: anyone who works hard can rise from humble (read here "marginal") origins and become successful and well-regarded. American business seems to revel in such stories.

Out of Conventionality

Some segments of the American population have had much easier access to achieved status than others. The European American middle class consists in large part of those who have "made it" and expect their children to do the same. Where, then, does middle-class life typically place the churches whose members inhabit it? Certainly not in marginality. Our discussions in earlier chapters should have led us to realize that members' economic stability often goes hand-in-glove with their church's conventional location on the grid. Conventionality, as we saw, does not lend itself naturally to a move of postures. Thus, the challenge here is to find a point of marginality and live in it. Social pressure in both blatant and subtle ways makes a congregation's move from conventionality to marginality strenuous.

In other words, most of today's churches—living in conventionality—are challenged by the contextual posture grid to seek an edge of somewhere and embrace its ambiguity and discomfort. As a pastor and a teacher of pastors, I do not think that this point can be emphasized too much. Those congregations who represent groups benefiting from achieved status now face the challenge to use their freedom in achieving to choose an edge. Since they already enjoy some degree of fitting into their world, they now must choose to live with a foot outside of that comfort zone. The choice is basically the same whether the church currently lives out of the inner-directed or the empathetic quadrant of conventionality. However, I do believe that it is more likely for those in empathy to have enough energy and honesty to move toward marginality. Since inner-directed conventionality is more common in our era, the challenge to move will call for significant effort and will affect the denominations whose churches are seeking greater witness.

This is not the same kind of trial that faces congregations who had no choice but to begin in marginality. Embracing the marginality that you have been given is much different than choosing from a position of conventionality a point of marginality toward which to move. White middle-class churches never can know just what it is like to be black or Asian or Hispanic in America, but they can choose to claim an edge for ministry, the embrace of which will require continual energy and commitment. That is my hope: that white churches especially will accept empathetic marginality as a prophetic, gospel calling.

The Edge and Renewal

So whether your church is EuroAmerican, African American, Asian or Hispanic American, or describable by any other category, a move into empathetic marginality by any congregation virtually assures that it is undergoing renewal. In the conditions in which we currently exist, it is very unlikely that a new church begins its life in empathetic marginality. I am hoping that more will do so in the future, but the weight of the past still bears much baggage from recent eras that favored conventionality. The energy required for a church to become both empathetic and marginal creates something new enough that the church clearly will not be the way that it was. Not all renewal will produce empathetic marginality, however. Renewal processes, the subject of a considerable amount of literature since about 1990, typically move congregations onto the empathy half of the grid. It is easier, as we have seen, to remain in conventionality than to claim an edge and move toward it.

Some congregations might decide that their decision to move toward empathetic marginality would be strengthened by resources designed for renewal. Any time a church is deliberate about its future, considerable issues and predictable resistances are at play. An outside coach, whether a book or skilled person, often will make the difference in moving successfully through anxiety, past resistance, and into the necessary early steps of accomplishment and change.

Leadership on the Edge

Congregations who reach empathetic marginality have been led there, and congregations who stay in empathetic marginality not only are still led but themselves generate leadership. In this book's middle chapters, I noted what kind of leadership each contextual posture depends on and what it needs to move. Yet I have left the larger discussion of leadership for this last chapter, because it is easy to misunderstand what leadership is and what it looks like.

Not Alone

Especially for congregations, it is easy to assume that leading is primarily the role of the pastor. I hope that the story of Trinity United Church of Christ helps to dispel this assumption. We have seen that, during the interim period between pastors, Trinity's church board agreed upon a statement that would guide its pastoral search. This statement articulated what the board wanted the church to pursue as its mission, in response to specific, significant changes in the world around it. The pastoral candidate who was presented to the congregation accepted the nomination on the basis of the search committee's commitment to follow this statement. Certainly the new pastor's influence was a key in Trinity initiating changes consistent with the statement. Initially, however, the struggle to redefine itself began at Trinity before the new pastor arrived. Working through this struggle is a mark of leading, and it needs to occur in community.

Thus, one of the important features of leading on the edge is that it is not a solo enterprise. During times of great religious movement, pastors do not dominate: they share leadership with lay persons, with women, with those of other ethnic backgrounds, and so on.[18] We are speaking here of something more than a wider diffusion of actual, formal organizational positions but of broad participation in creating and implementing new ideas. Empathetic marginal congregations come to realize and benefit from this kind of "multiple leadership."[19] It has long-lasting effects, one of which is inspiring competent, experienced church members to expand their vocations. This certainly has been the case with Trinity United Church of Christ. In Pastor Jeremiah Wright's first 25 years as pastor, the congregation sponsored about fifty of its members in graduate theological training.[20] Having taught a number of these members myself, I can attest to their capabilities and their understanding of ministry as a shared venture.

Marginality and Leading

Reviewing the basic qualities of empathetic marginality high-lights what we mean and do not mean by "leadership." If marginality means being in some way at odds with the wider world, then leadership itself must have a marginal quality to it. Biblical examples abound. Jacob's favored son, Joseph, lived out of at least three different forms of marginality during his lifetime: first, as his father's pet; second, as Pharoah's prisoner; and third, as Pharoah's governor (yes, even high privilege is a form of marginality). Moses's social status in his day also moved from one marginal extreme to another. He began as a Hebrew baby under an edict of death; he was raised in Pharoah's court but became a fugitive after committing murder; then he thought his life was secure as a shepherd for his father-in-law; finally, Moses was called by God to return to Egypt and lead his people out of slavery. Jesus himself was a marginal Jew, raised in Galilee—considered a backwater district in which Jews mingled with the hated half-breed Samaritans. The apostle Paul lived on more than one edge as well: being a Pharisee among the Jews, this early Christian missionary also held the high status of Roman citizenship.

Scriptural witness to marginality hence demonstrates its social, economic, political, and cultural dimensions. These categories are at play in today's world as well, and they affect institutions and churches, and the individuals who constitute them. This means that leadership—especially as we think about it for empathetic marginality—functions as it takes into account the ways that society, economics, politics, culture (and even religion) are used to push people to margins. Ironically, many of today's congregations grew up in a time when it was easy for them to be conventional. Extensive research on religion in American society over the last two decades clearly concludes that these days have gone.[21] Therefore, it can be argued that many existing congregations have little choice left but to find a way to live from an edge.[22]

Empathy and Leading

By itself, however, marginality will not be a cutting edge. It depends upon empathy to provide it the energy to move to the edge of somewhere, rather than living in the middle of nowhere. To make this move is to see leadership at work. Yet empathy in congregational culture does not come naturally. Look at its most dramatic biblical parallel, the use of an unusual Greek word to describe Jesus's feelings as he engaged in ministry. That word, σπλαγνιζομαι, "splagnizomai," is commonly translated into English as "to have compassion." It is a strong verb that appears hardly a dozen times in the New Testament, all in the Synoptic Gospels (i.e., Matthew, Mark, and Luke).[23] Three times, this verb is used in parables, those that we commonly name the Good Samaritan (Luke 10:33), the Prodigal Son (Luke 15:20) and the Unforgiving Servant (Matthew 18:27). Virtually all the other references are in stories in which Jesus heals someone or feeds large crowds. The Samaritan "has compassion" for the robbery and beating victim on the road; the father "has compassion" for the son who returns home after squandering his share of the inheritance; a king "had compassion" on one of his slaves who owed him money; Jesus "had compassion" on a leper, a boy with a spirit, two blind men, a widow's son, and the crowds who listened to his teaching and needed to eat.

All of these uses of the Greek verb "splagnizo" appear in stories or episodes in which a basic human need is evident. At the heart of compassion is the capacity to empathize, to "feel with" the struggles and difficult circumstances of someone else or another group. People who empathize tend to be more magnanimous; they think beyond themselves and are willing to share what they have in order to help alleviate the hardship of another. By itself, however, having empathy does not mean that one is leading. For religious communities, empathy does indeed stir believers to care enough about others to share. When that caring becomes wed to a vision of a better world (in one way or another),[24] empathy can lead. When empathy is driven by a vision that calls for the community to live on an edge, it creates leadership in marginality.

Accepting Tension

Leading in empathetic marginality, therefore, illustrates the double tension that creates this congregational posture in the first place. For one thing, empathy requires deliberate attention in order to sustain its altruistic strength; this attention tugs against the common human tendency to be interested mainly in oneself. For another thing, marginality requires deliberate attention to the congregation's place in its world. It is never an accident that a marginal church (whether by condition or by choice) chooses to live from its edge. One of the dangers to maintaining marginality creatively is in the congregation neglecting to assess on a regular basis the conditions of its context and its actual relationship to that context. Ministry can and does occur outside of marginality, but it will not be ministry that embodies the "new thing" (Isaiah 43:18-19). Marginality that remains empathetic continues to lean into the ambiguity, the risk, and the relative insecurity of living on an edge.

The Edge and the Center

Let us be clear, however, that authentic leadership (as distinguished from impressive initiative) does not portray circumstances and opportunities in simplistic, either-or terms. Empathetic marginality is not a withdrawal from the world, as the utopian communities in early American life practiced or contemporary cults require.[25] The strength of this congregational posture derives in part from internal resources (mature faith, life experience, trusting relationships, education, and other skills) that are drawn upon to link up with external resources in the very world with which the congregation stays on some edge. This dynamic in itself underscores the tension of empathetic marginal witness. Churches in this posture are more able and willing to recognize the ways in which they themselves participate in the world's struggles that have led them to choose an edge.

What this means for leadership is that it does not have a simple or easily predictable look. Trinity United Church of Christ, for instance, pulls no punches in continuing to define and express an Africentric way of being Christian in the United States. One of its strategies for meeting this mission is by educating its members. On the one hand, Trinity wants its teenagers to do well in school and pursue careers as part of their Christian vocation. On the other hand, Trinity operates its own extensive Christian education program, which is Africentric, offering in part a critique of certain values and behaviors in American society.[26] Trinity members and the congregation as a whole do not disengage from the world around them, but they do challenge it on matters of racism and inequality. Their ministry posture and style illustrates what Lovett Weems means by leading from both the edge and the center.[27] Empathetic marginal churches do not conclude naïvely that living on an edge means ignoring or despising conventional realities; instead, they have learned how to "be wise as serpents and innocent as doves" (Matthew 10:16). As Weems says, "the concept of living *both* at the center *and* the edge is closer to the reality of New Testament people."[28]

Qualities of Edge Leadership

As you begin to think about what it would take for your church to live out of empathetic marginality, you might wonder what characteristics would need to be nurtured in order for the church's members—with their pastor—to lead. Posing this question highlights my premise that leadership itself is a particular kind of thing, sometimes misunderstood in our American emphasis upon pragmatic action. In themselves, getting things done and "making people do what you want" are not examples of leading. Instead, leadership always centers in some way around expressing and pursuing a vision for the community in question.[29] In order for any congregation to take the leap into empathetic marginality, it must identify its calling from God, its vision. Any process that eventuates in clarity of shared vision will exhibit leadership, as will the activities undertaken to fulfill that vision.

I have discussed leadership in some detail elsewhere,[30] informed by the wisdom of others. The earlier chapters in this book have implied that not all forms of leadership will look the same, since the circumstances and needs in each contextual posture are different. At the same time, however, the ability to lead tends to be supported by an array of qualities that seem to be common among those who genuinely lead. Let us consider a few of these here.

First, empathetic marginality emerges from, and also fosters in those within the congregation's orbit, the key qualities of *personal growth, self-understanding, and competence in navigating and negotiating with others*. The community reflectiveness that is necessary for a church to move into (and remain in) empathetic marginality stimulates self-examination among the church's members. It is not possible to maintain both the empathetic reach and the marginal stance without maintaining and utilizing the capacity for persons to be aware of self and skilled with other people.

A second closely related leadership quality is the *ability and willingness to learn*. Our American society often behaves as though it expects its "leaders" to know what to do already, to have "all the answers." In a world of such rapid change, this is a naïve and sometimes foolish assumption. People who are prepared to lead are those who can recognize what they do not know and what the group does not know that is affecting the pursuit of their purpose. Sometimes this will mean getting information in statistical and demographic form; other times it will mean listening to certain constituents in a way that the church or member has not listened previously. A congregation choosing to live out of marginality must remain a learner.

Willingness to learn implies, third, a *humble spirit*. Those who act like they already know it all are much less likely to admit what they do not know—which means that they probably do not know themselves and others as well as they think they do. Empathetic churches living out of marginality depend upon tension between the empathy and the marginality to keep themselves humble.

When these three qualities are at work in a congregation and its members, eventually a fourth quality appears—that of *courage*. Americans often seem to mistake courage for ambition or some sort of assertive enterprise. Courage weighs the risks involved— even the risk from what the church does not know—with the pursuit of a goal that helps fulfill vision. Courage takes a good risk for a worthy cause. Empathetic marginal churches learn how to name their fears as well as their hopes, so that their courage serves in part to keep them on that edge where their vision can bloom.

Living on an edge with a full heart does not happen to a church overnight. One of the foundations of this critical church posture for the future is pastors and members with *experience in liminality*. By this we refer to times and episodes in a person's life in which they had to function outside of their familiar world but did not feel settled in another one. Liminality is a real and strong phenomenon, and opportunities to experience it in many ways will multiply with the complex shifts of the twenty-first century world. When someone travels to a place where they have not been before, they drink from the waters of liminality, even if only for a brief period. Working a summer job in another state, going to college across the country, a city dweller spending the summer on an uncle's farm, working in an office where you are a minority in some way—these and other scenarios set up circumstances that create for the person a time of being "betwixt and between." Persons who have lived through "not fitting in," and allowed themselves to learn something beneficial from it, are better prepared to lead in an empathetic marginal church.

A Church for the Future

The impetus for this book grew out of my extended ruminations on the role of Christian communities in the life of the world. These musings reflect a journey of their own, and I hope that reading this book has prompted in you a new appreciation and interpretation of your own reflections. My own experience reveals patterns that are observable in collective human experience and that can be identified, measured, and predicted. As scientists develop theories to explain things that we observe in nature, I offer the contextual posture grid as a way to help church folks explain what they see going on in their congregations.

Yet you know that I am interested in much more than mere explanation. Knowing why something is happening is useful only if we do something with what we discover. Otherwise, we are like the one who hears the word but does not do it, who gazes at the mirror's reflection but walks away and forgets what they saw (James 1:23-24). The ideas in this book point us in some directions and assess some of the benefits and limitations of those directions. Most centrally, Christian witness in the world of the upcoming future will hardly allow for a wholesale withdrawal or complacency.

Instead, let us challenge ourselves as followers of the Way. Let us be brave enough to hear what the gospel sounds like when we are standing on a street corner downtown and not only in the security of a beautiful sanctuary. Let us find ways in our congregations to begin our journeys afresh, neither by plunging into a resistance of despair nor by letting the bull loose in the china shop. I believe that the transforming and liberating power of the Holy Spirit can do marvelous things, even in the midst of church folks who are scared, tepid, or overindulged. I believe that a congregation's path of faith witness can take unexpected and wonderful turns, even though so many churches have no idea or motivation to risk their comfort in Jesus's name.

Let us, therefore, call ourselves to account. The needs and opportunities are great; God has blessed us and will bless us even more. Our spiritual ancestors in the Scriptures show us the way. May the ideas in this book inspire you and your congregation to become a church on the edge of somewhere.

Notes

1. Elizabeth O'Connor, *Call to Commitment* (New York: Harper & Row, 1963) and *Journey Inward, Journey Outward* (New York: Harper & Row, 1968).
2. Again see Timothy L. Smith, *Revivalism and Social Reform: American Protestantism on the Eve of the Civil War* (New York: Harper & Row, 1957), 44.
3. Ibid., 59.
4. Ibid., 92–93.
5. Ibid., 80–84.
6. Ibid., 148.
7. See Max Weber, "The Nature of Charismatic Domination," in *Weber: Selections in Translation*, edited by W.G. Runciman, translated by Eric Matthews, (Cambridge: Cambridge University Press, 1978), 226–250, esp. 231, 236–238, 245, and 247.
8. Lovett H. Weems, Jr., *Leadership in the Wesleyan Spirit* (Nashville: Abingdon Press, 1999), 72–74.

9. Timothy Smith pointed out that the pre–Civil War revival met its strongest opposition among "Old School Presbyterians, High Church Episcopalians, and Confessional Lutherans." See Smith, op.cit., 85.

10. See Weems, op.cit., ch. 6.

11. Kirk Hadaway and David Roozen, *Rerouting the Protestant Mainstream: Sources of Hope and Opportunities for Change* (Nashville: Abingdon Press, 1995), 91–92.

12. Ibid., 93–95.

13. Ibid., 102–103.

14. Ibid., 110–112.

15. Ibid., 114–116.

16. For an extended discussion of the theory of cultural confluence, see my *How to Get Along with Your Pastor: Creating Partnership for Doing Ministry* (Cleveland: The Pilgrim Press, 2006), ch. 3.

17. I discuss this kind of "bad news" process in my *How to Get Along with Your Church: Creating Cultural Capital for Doing Ministry* (Cleveland: The Pilgrim Press, 2001), ch. 4; the primary audience for this book is pastors, but the overall process is discussed there.

18. This point has been made already in reference to Timothy Smith's *Revivalism and Social Reform*. See also a similar point made by Lovett Weems in *Leadership in the Wesleyan Spirit*, 70.

19. A term used by Weems; see *Leadership in the Wesleyan Spirit*, 70.

20. Author's telephone conversation with the Rev. Dr. Jeremiah Wright, September 1997.

21. This literature is extensive. Much of its findings are summarized in Hadaway and Roozen, op.cit., ch. 1, esp. 33–35.

22. See Weems, op.cit., 76–78.

23. See Walter Bauer, *A Greek-English Lexicon of the New Testament and Other Early Christian Literature*, English edition revised by F. Wilbur Gingrich and Frederick W. Danker from Bauer's fifth edition, (Chicago: University of Chicago Press, 1958), 762.

24. Vision is central to leadership. For a general discussion of vision, its purposes and benefits, see Weems, *Church Leadership: Vision, Culture, Team, Integrity* (Nashville: Abingdon Press, 1993), ch. 2. For a process of discerning congregational vision, see my *Futuring Your Church: Finding Your Vision and Making It Work* (Cleveland:

The Pilgrim Press, 1999), esp. ch. 7, "Moving Ahead—Making Your Vision Work."

25. A brief discussion of factors contributing to nineteenth-century utopian movements, as well as summaries of four of them, is found in Winthrop S. Hudson and John Corrigan, *Religion in America,* 5th ed. (New York: Macmillan, 1992), 181–187. Historically recent groups such as the People's Temple in Guyana and the Branch Davidians in Waco, Texas, are memorable primarily because of their bizarre, violent demises. What they had in common with the earlier utopians movements, however, was a conviction that the only way to satisfy God's expectation for righteous, faithful living was to withdraw from society in general.

26. William R. Myers describes this kind of youth ministry in his report on research of an affluent white church and a middle-class black church, in which the black church teaches its youth to question the wider society. See his *Black and White Styles of Youth Ministry: Two Congregations in America,* foreword by Thomas Kochman, introduction by Charles R. Foster (New York: The Pilgrim Press, 1991), esp. ch. 8.

27. See Weems, *Leadership in the Wesleyan Spirit,* 78–81.

28. Ibid., 79.

29. For discussions of this link between leadership and vision, considered for church context, see Lovett Weems, *Church Leadership,* esp. 54–61; see also elaboration of Weem's ideas in *How to Get Along with Your Church,* 76–77, 80–81. A congregational-centered process for discerning vision can be found in my *Futuring Your Church.*

30. George B. Thompson, Jr., editor and contributor, *Alligators in the Swamp: Power, Ministry and Leadership* (Cleveland: The Pilgrim Press, 2005), esp. ch. 6, "Reflections on Ministry Practice and Leadership," and ch. 2, "Self and Dressing for the Swamp," the latter coauthored with Beverly Thompson; see also my *How to Get Along with Your Pastor,* ch. 7.